Of the two Japanese poets presented here, and the others who, like himself, survived World War Two, Ōoka Makoto writes: "In addition to living with vivid memories of war horrors . . . most poets also had to fight off poverty and hunger on a daily basis. This made all the stronger their desire to find in poetry a kind of spiritual salvation. . . . Thus the fruitful union of strong social criticism and surreal images . . . the inseparable union of lyricism and cultural criticism."

Yoshioka Minoru, born 1919 and still a strong influence on younger writers, is a modest man and an elegant, often baffling poet who rejects all taboos to bring into Japanese poetry what he sees as a "celebration in darkness, at once weird and refined, scatalogical and lofty, comical and serious."

Iijima Kōichi, born 1930, was only 15 when the two atomic bombs provided the Japanese with a vision, as Ōoka Makoto puts it, "of apocalypse utterly without divine presence." Unimpressed by a postwar prosperity he believes is based on a circus of consummer manipulation, he wanders an area where rationality and fantasy overlap, and drily reports on what he sees.

By bringing together in one volume the work of these two very different yet deeply similar poets we hope to throw into sharp relief the qualities of each while suggesting the range of poetry being written in Japan.

Celebration In Darkness

Strangers' Sky

Asian Poetry in Translation: Japan #6

Asian Poetry in Translation: Japan
Editor, Thomas Fitzsimmons

This project is supported by a grant from the National Endowment for the Arts.

Celebration In Darkness
Selected Poems of YOSHIOKA MINORU

Strangers' Sky
Selected Poems of IIJIMA KŌICHI

Translated by Onuma Tadayoshi

Introduction by Ōoka Makoto

Commentary on the poets by Tsuruoka Yoshihisa

KATYDID BOOKS
Oakland University   Rochester, Michigan   1985

103511

First Edition

Book design, cover and illustrations by Karen Hargreaves-Fitzsimmons

Calligraphy by the authors

Japanese text reproduced with the kind permission of Shichōsha Publishing Co. and Seidosha Publishing Co. of Tokyo

Produced by K T DID Productions

Printed in the United States of America on acid free paper by McNaughton & Gunn, Saline, Michigan
Set in Bembo by Sans Serif Typesetters, Ann Arbor, Michigan

Library of Congress Cataloging in Publication Data

Yoshioka, Minoru, 1919–
    Celebration in darkness.

    (Asian poetry in translation. Japan ; 6)
    Japanese text, parallel English translation.
    1. Japanese poetry — 20th century — Translations into English. 2. English poetry — Translations from Japanese. 3. Yoshioka, Minoru, 1919–   — Translations, English. 4. Iijima, Kōichi, 1930–
— Translations, English. I. Onuma, Tadayoshi, 1943–   . II. Ōoka, Makoto, 1931–   . III. Tsuruoka, Yoshihisa, 1936–   . IV. Iijima, Kōichi, 1930–   . Strangers' sky. 1985. V. Title. VI. Title: Strangers' sky.

PL782.E3Y6 1985   895.6'15'08   84-23423
ISBN 0-942668-07-3 (soft)

Celebration In Darkness

Strangers' Sky

Contents

STRANGERS' SKY

Commentary   75

The Poems

The Japanese poems begin at the far end of the book and move toward the center in the normal Japanese manner.

All Japanese names are given in the Japanese order—family name first.

Introduction

Modern Japanese Poetry — Realities and Challenges

By Ōoka Makoto

Written poetry in Japan has a history of more than thirteen centuries. The first great Japanese poet, Kakinomoto Hitomaro, wrote during the last two decades of the seventh century. His poems are included along with those of several hundred other known and anonymous ancient poets in the *Man'yōshū* (*Collection for Myriad Ages*), an anthology containing 4,516 poems in all—poems that are even today widely read and studied. A dozen or so major works—monographs, exegeses, commentaries, essays—on the *Man'yōshū* appear annually and some of them sell exceptionally well.

In how many countries is a poetic form that was perfected more than a thousand years ago not only the object of extremely specialized research but also avidly read by people in all walks of life? This phenomenon reflects an important characteristic of modern Japanese culture as a whole. Modern Japan contains any number of delicate fusions of ancient and modern in its arts, politics, and social dynamics. When, for example, a large electronics firm using state-of-the-art technology constructs a new factory, the ground-breaking ceremony is presided over by a Shinto priest who recites and sings ancient charms and incantations believed to have the power to purify the construction site. This kind of juxtaposition of old and new can be seen in so many aspects of daily life in modern Japan that the Japanese are often not aware of them.

The imperial family itself was originally the highest-ranking priestly clan overseeing state rituals. The imperial court was and continues to be the largest and most carefully kept repository of ancient ritual and incantation, although in considerably polished and edited form. In fact, the history of the Waka, the dominant form of court poetry for centuries, is inseparable from the history of a series of prestigious court anthologies, each edited in the name of the then-reigning emperor. The first of these imperial anthologies was the *Kokinshū* (*Ancient and Modern Collection*), which was completed in about 905. Twenty more followed it in the next five centuries or so. These imperial anthologies—especially the *Kokinshū* and the *Shinkokinshū* (*New Ancient and Modern Collection*), which was completed in 1206—achieved unsurpassed heights of refined beauty that have left a permanent and incalculable influence on subsequent Japanese culture.

The courtly tradition, like all others, eventually lost its vision and vigor. Then in the late 19th century, when Japan began its rapid process of Westernization, the Waka (now usually called Tanka, or "short song") also underwent swift and wrenching changes. It left forever the sphere of courtly values and came to be written by ordinary people, people who used it to express new feelings and perspectives in strikingly new ways. The Tanka form was renovated, not abandoned; crisis resulted in renaissance.

Amazingly, the ancient Tanka form came to be used expressively and subtly by a number of outstanding modern poets. The form continues to grow in popularity, and it is presently used by at least a million Japanese. The brevity of the Tanka makes it very effective as occasional verse—for capturing the fleeting yet permanently moving emotions evoked by the small events of everyday life. This continued life and development of the Tanka is a major reason why modern Japanese readers and poets continue to be passionately drawn to the ancient *Man'yōshū* anthology.

The standard Tanka contains only thirty-one syllables, which fall into five rhythmic units or "lines" of 5, 7, 5, 7 and 7 syllables. One poetic form, however, is even shorter than the Tanka. Originally called Haikai, it is now referred to as haiku. In the Japanese medieval period the first three lines of the Tanka developed into an independent 17-syllable form having three lines of 5, 7, and 5 syllables. Haiku were originally linked together in sequences, but in the late 19th century they, like the Tanka, were the subject of intense Western-stimulated reform and experimentation and soon developed into self-sufficient poems standing by themselves. As a result of this haiku renaissance, the modern haiku form is fully as popular as the modern Tanka. It is appealing above all because of its extreme brevity, which requires suggestion rather than statement. The haiku lover is also a lover of silence.

To give foreign readers some sense of what these two traditional forms are actually like, I would like to quote a Tanka and a haiku by Masaoka Shiki (1867–1902), a poet who played a major role in the modernization of both. Although Shiki died of pulmonary tuberculosis when he was only thirty-five, his creatively militant theories and the examples of his own poems were the single greatest reforming influence on traditional Japanese poetry. Although Shiki was confined to his bed for the last six years of his life by spinal tuberculosis, his creative power and energy lasted until the very end. In addition to Tanka and haiku, Shiki also kept a journal during his last years which ranks as one of the masterpieces of early modern Japanese prose.

One winter day Shiki heard voices exclaiming that it was snowing outside—a rare sight. Since he was unable to get up and go see the snow, Shiki wrote a haiku instead:

> Again and again
> I ask how deep
> the snow

As in most haiku, the poet's own feeling is not directly expressed. Yet Japanese readers can feel deep within this extremely reticent poem the bedridden poet's desperate, irrepressible curiosity and longing to see the falling snow and can sympathize and feel pity at the snow drifting through Shiki's heart.

Another day, Shiki lay watching the early summer flowers that were blooming in his small garden. Filled with a premonition that his death was not far away, he wrote ten Tanka to the flowers as if to say goodbye to each of them. One of them:

> Iris petals
> begin to open—
> the last spring
> I will ever see
> almost gone

The Tanka form, because it is somewhat more spacious than the haiku, allows the poet to state or develop an emotion: it is essentially lyric. In Shiki's Tanka, the rebirth of a small flower in his garden contrasts poignantly with his own sense of impending death. His love of the flower makes his own life seem all the more precious and all the harder to leave behind. Yet both the Tanka and the haiku value reticence and indirect suggestion to a degree perhaps unequaled in other poetic traditions.

In the vortex of contending theories and styles that overtook late 19th-century Japan, a new poetic form emerged that had no relation to either the Tanka or the haiku: colloquial free verse. A number of outstanding free-verse poets soon began writing about things and themes that could not be expressed in the shorter traditional forms.

When the Tokugawa shogunate, which had ruled Japan for two and a half centuries, was overthrown in 1868, one of the first acts of the new Meiji regime was to reverse the closed-door policy toward other nations that had been in effect since 1635. The new Japanese rulers, alarmed by the expansionist policies of Europe, Russia, and the United States, threw themselves behind a crash program of Westernization in order to keep Japan from becoming another colony of one of the Western powers. Ironically, however, in their effort to "catch up" with the West, Japan's rulers created a European-style absolutist state of their own. Thus the Japan of the late 19th and early 20th centuries was an explosive mixture of rapid imitation of Western models on the one hand and reactionary nationalism—including colonization of surrounding areas of Asia—on the other.

Poetry, of course, was also torn in different directions at once. Yet free verse was able to hold its own. More and more young poets began to write it, and translations of Western poetry grew in quality and quantity. Growing numbers of readers, dissatisfied with the Tanka and the haiku, also began to passionately read and discuss free verse, thus laying the foundation for the next generation of free-verse poets. The free verse written before World War Two, however, is usually distinguished from that written after 1945. Japan's military defeat had very large repercussions in every part of its society and culture, and postwar Japanese poetry differs markedly from its predecessors. Japanese free-verse poetry written between 1945 and around 1960 is often referred to as "postwar" poetry. In relation to the Tanka and the haiku, however, free verse written from 1945 to the present is usually called "modern" poetry.

Free verse, now entering its second century in Japan, was from the beginning influenced in various ways by new Western trends and movements, from romanticism and symbolism in the 19th century to dada and surrealism in the 20th. Japanese literary criticism was also deeply influenced. In fact, it is impossible to describe modern Japanese literary criticism without mentioning its connections with French symbolist theory. In poetry the links were even closer.

Many of the Western influences were not, however, unambiguous. When, as has happened so often in history, the spiritual and intellectual products of a more highly articulated and developed cultural area move across boundaries into a less sophisticated area, changes in form and quality occur, since the less developed area must assimilate the foreign influences within the configurations of its own traditions and perspectives. The poets and scholars of ancient Japan, for example, revered the larger civilization of China and worked strenuously to understand and adopt it, yet they always chose with great care what they imported and how they imported it. Thus the great T'ang-period poets Li Po and Tu Fu were not widely read in Japan because these poets often expressed great anger at political conditions and their own personal situation, condemning and even cursing a whole range of public targets—all subjects frowned on at the Japanese court of the 10th and 11th centuries. It was the milder Po Chü-i who became the most read and loved Chinese poet in Japan. But it was only the nostalgic Po musing on the beauties of nature who became so popular; all of the political poems full of righteous anger and admonition by Po the advisor and Minister of Justice were carefully edited out of Japanese editions. Li Po, Tu Fu, and even Po Chü-i were not fully understood and did not exert a deep influence until the late 17th century, when Matsuo Bashō wrote. Bashō's own life and poetry allowed—and required—him to grasp this neglected side of the Chinese poets.

A somewhat similar situation arose when Japanese poetry collided with Western poetry in the process of Japanese Westernization. This is why 1945 is such a crucial dividing line.

The year 1945 brought many new experiences to the Japanese. It was, first of all, the first experience of defeat for Japan as a nation-state. Second, it was the year the nuclear age began with two unspeakably destructive atomic bombs being exploded over Hiroshima and Nagasaki. Third, it was the year the militarism and fanaticism that had ruled Japan since the early 1930s were militarily crushed and the ultranationalistic ideology that had supported the militarist system was discredited and destroyed. Fourth, it was the year the Allies occupied Japan and instituted American-style democracy, setting off far-reaching changes in the Japanese political, economic, and social systems, symbolized by the establishment of a new national constitution. The reorganization of the Japanese educational system during the American occupation is a striking example of how traditional Japanese society was shaken to its foundations. Fifth, 1945 was the year of burned-out cities, hunger, black markets, homeless children, the wounded, and almost every other kind of hardship—a situation that did not improve until the economy began to recover during the Korean War. Eliot's *The Waste Land* and Auden's *The Age of Anxiety* seemed to many Japanese titles that summed up their own country. And wars of many kinds continued to break out, in China, in Korea, in Algeria, in Hungary, in Cuba, and on and on.

In 1945 I was fourteen. I still remember clearly how, during the years after that, I and many of my anxious generation felt not so much that we were living in the postwar period as that we had now entered the prewar period before World War Three. Most of the poems I wrote when I was around twenty, even the love poems, also deal with this "prewar" world. In this I was far from being alone.

These, then, were some of the elements haunting Japan's so-called "postwar" poetry. War experiences, hunger, atomic bombs—they and much more engraved themselves in the minds of Japanese poets and made death a central and commonly used image. But by experiencing global war and nuclear destruction Japanese poets also learned to view personal tragedies as tragedies on a world scale, a perspective denied to Japanese poets writing before World War Two. Now Japanese poets were forced, whether they wanted to or not, to look through their individual fates and see the fate of the whole 20th century. Only after World War Two was Japanese poetry ready to absorb concretely the real meaning of European movements such as dada, surrealism, expressionism, Neue Sachlichkeit, and existentialism. Most of these movements arose after World War One and had been known and discussed in Japan during the 1920s and 30s, but it was only after the Japanese experienced nuclear war, rubble, and hunger that the real force of these movements came home to them. It was the same kind of process the poems of Li Po, Tu Fu, and Po Chü-i had had to pass through, only this time the gap was shorter.

And it was only after World War Two that the basic attitudes and concepts expressed in Paul Valery's cultural criticism, T.S. Eliot's *The Waste Land*, André Breton and Philippe Soupault's *Les champs magnétiques*, Breton and Paul Éluard's *L'Immaculée Conception*, and similar works made sense in Japan and evoked a profound, sympathetic response.

Behind this sympathy lay the new conviction that poetry was an alternative to religion and science that could successfully resist the devastation, mass death, and despair surrounding the modern world. No matter how optimistic this belief may seem now, postwar Japanese poetry could not have set out without it, because when the Japanese experienced two atomic bombs they also witnessed, symbolically, a vision of apocalypse utterly without divine presence. This is why the demand "Bring back totality through poetry" was common to every group and trend in postwar Japan until at least the 1960s.

Technically, postwar Japanese poetry became incomparably more conscious of itself, raising sense to the level of thought and embodying thought at the level of sense. Greater attention was paid to metaphor and imagery, but the heightened interest in technique was above all a part of the demand for the restoration of totality through poetry. In addition to having to live with vivid memories of war horrors—experienced on the Asian mainland, the South Pacific, in Japan itself— most poets also had to fight off poverty and hunger on a daily basis. This made all the stronger their desire to find in poetry a kind of spiritual salvation—their desire to make poetry responsible for expressing their dream of totality. Thus the fruitful union of strong social criticism and surreal images in the poems of the major postwar poets. Thus the inseparable union of lyricism and cultural criticism. A poet, in other words, also had to be a penetrating critic. Throughout the history of

Japanese poetry, from ancient times until the end of the 19th century, almost every major poet was also a powerful critic. In fact, it was not until around 1920, and for a short time after, that criticism and poetry were regarded as adversaries.

In any case, modern poetry, as an alternative to science and religion, was now required to restore a fundamental unity and totality to human thought and action. This was the great claim made by postwar Japanese poetry.

For poetry, what is the modern age?

For our age, what meaning does poetry have?

Both questions are, of course, very difficult to answer. They are made all the more difficult by the fact that each question intertwines with the other in extremely dark and subtle ways. Yet poets have to ask these questions every moment they are poets. The incredible advances made by modern science and the violent social changes they bring about—changes that affect the smallest corners of our daily life—make the answers even harder to find.

Science, the brilliant weapon for conquering poverty, ignorance, superstition, and suffering; science, which developed as the advance guard for opposing and overcoming absolutism, tyranny, and oppression; this same science now dares to pursue not only nuclear fission and fusion but even genetic engineering and artificial brain-cell expansion. These experiments, of course, can easily turn into destructive attacks on the very basis of human life. The gigantic dual potential and contradictions inherent in science symbolize the central dilemma now faced by humanity as a whole. Yet it is impossible to conceive of a future without science. Neither can the poet ignore it.

In the 1970s science brought to Japan, as elsewhere, new electronic technologies including everything from photocopy and video equipment to vending machines and procedures that make possible the immediate copying and large-scale dissemination and circulation of something which was momentarily known as an "original." Poetry cannot help but be influenced by this historical trend. What is called the "copy civilization" or "copy society" in Japan takes from the hands of the poet poems that were written in a non-reproducible realm of experience and almost instantly spreads them indiscriminately in every direction. Radical thinning and weakening is inevitable. Even the concept of originality, which underlies so many myths about poetry, is in urgent need of reconsideration.

But there is hope for modern poetry precisely because the age is so complex: because humans possess words, live by means of words, live words, are words themselves. Since words are the basic bond holding together and making possible history and society, poetry—which exists in order to search for the most fundamental ways and usages of words—finds in crisis the profoundest of all reasons to go beyond itself and live as it has never done before.

Translated by Christopher Drake
Tokyo, 1984

Celebration In Darkness
Yoshioka Minoru

Yoshioka Minoru—
"Celebration In Darkness. . . ."

by Tsuruoka Yoshihisa

Yoshioka Minoru was born on April 15th, 1919. The years from 1941 to 1945 he spent as a soldier in the Pacific War. The first collection of his poems was compiled and edited in two days when he received the summons to the colors. Entitled *Liquid*, this book came out on December 10th, 1941, and the author received his copies on an arctic battlefield in Manchuria. The only book to come out of Yoshioka's twenties, *Liquid* is in more than one sense a memento of his adolescence.

Yoshioka's early poems were distinctly colored by the Japanese modernist movement (which flourished around such central figures as Kitazono Katsue and Haruyama Yukio) of the latter half of the 1920s. *Liquid* thus features poems at once lyrical and surrealist.

> Pull out from under a tree on a festival day of the Blessed Virgin
> Parenthesize a desert into the brain's afternoon. . .

Every poem in *Liquid* is a series of *non sequiturs* devoid of any "story," and this tendency is carried forward into Yoshioka's later poems which will no doubt resist translation more than any other Japanese poet's. Yoshioka's poems are aggregates of magical images produced by an aesthetic consciousness which is well-nigh esoteric.

In "How I Write Poems?" Yoshioka tells us how his poems come into being.

> I start my poems with no premeditated themes or structures. For me a blank sheet of paper is always the best place for poetry. . . . I become calmly saturated with a certain consciousness and a certain composition, and reality is established. Then come moments of white heat. I'm visited with ennui, and then by despair. I see a certain painting. A female body is imagined. I touch a substance hard as a tortoise-shell. A man who has been walking on planks goes away. Next float up the shape of a perambulator and the two Chinese characters for "vegetable". . .

Judging from this, Yoshioka's method is not very far from automatic writing, his pen moving to catch alive spontaneous images stirring in the stream of his consciousness.

Still Life was published in 1955, and *Monk* in 1958. This latter established Yoshioka Minoru as one of the most important Japanese poets today. In it what lies at the unfathomable bottom of everyday life is scooped up and crystalized by means of a poetic language which has enhanced its hardness considerably.

> . . . a royal road the still-born child will open
> into a primeval virgin land
> and there he will see
> the future delivery scene
> the maternal lightning torn open
> & from that immense bloody darkness out will come
> white-haired still-born children one after the other. . .
>
> "Still-Born"

Yoshioka's "war experience" is doubtless what lies behind these lines: his own words refer to them as "the first of its kind among my poems in which I tried, in my own fashion, to get involved with the outside world." But it is not the actualities of that world, such as might have been encountered by the poet during the war, for example, that are approached here. Rather, this world described is an irrational one (somehow reminiscent of nothingness itself) of a "mother" and her "still-born child" who are irrevocably estranged from everything that is alive. Perhaps in Yoshioka's eyes the inhumanity experienced during the war and the "false" peace of the postwar period were judged to be on a par. Here is a tragedy found to be persisting from the "primeval" times and far into the "future." The "white-haired still-born child" born out of "that immense bloody darkness" of "torn" maternity represents the poet's line of vision, if somewhat grotesque, refusing to be reconciled to the actualities of the world. Perhaps *Monk* can be viewed as a concentrated linguistic warfare in which Yoshioka tried to dispose *en masse* of the lyrical modernism and the "war experience" that were within himself. Everywhere in *Monk* we meet bitter humor and almost secret love for man and his world. And we now realize that this love or eroticism is what has enabled Yoshioka to break fresh poetic ground. The enmity long harbored against the world, and perhaps also against the poet's own being, now receding to a vanishing point, Yoshioka's poetry obtains a rhythm quite relieved and free together with a certain velocity.

In *Quiet House* (pub. 1968) the above tendency is still more apparent.

    I always think of that
    Soft horror of a door knob
    What is a stay?
    Look at a huge musical instrument popping open at a scene of a fire
    Ridicule I shall not
    What is not to be seen
    A woman's waist in my arms I go sliding
    The circle that circles shun
    There is a sausage coming back along its circuit
    After dividing up all realities
    It is a new conception. . .

                                                            "Stay"

The "soft horror of a door knob" speaks very well the characteristic feature of this volume. Formerly, Yoshioka's horror was stiff and stood upright in the dark, much like a knife of ice. Here, however, horror has turned into a soft knob, just like the limp clock of a Salvador Dali. Bright streams of light shine into these poems now, as if our poet is allowed to "stay" in the world that he has long been repulsing. Perhaps a certain "postwar surgery" has been successfully concluded in Yoshioka Minoru. Another thing that merits mention here is Yoshioka's marriage (his earnest love for his wife Yōko is well-known) which coincided with the writing of the poems included in the present volume. There have been numerous cases, Éluard's for one, where the presence of a female played a vital role in calling poetry into being. "A woman's waist in my arms I go sliding/The circle that circles shun. . ."—these lines seem to exude a very healthy kind of eroticism. We also find a sort of solidarity consciousness quickening in *Quiet House*, and this is in such a striking contrast to the sense of desolation which marked *Monk*. Here is how "Stay" ends:

> I think of that
> Tiny love under the umbrella
> The driving wheel of a speeding car
> Veering more and more sharply to the left. . .

This fresh "love" and this velocity: from here Yoshioka's poetry inaugurates its new development.

Saffron Gathering (pub. 1976) won the Takami Jun Prize (which is annually awarded to the best collection of poems of the year), and this occupies by far the most important place in the whole of Yoshioka Minoru's poetical achievements.

> . . . And yet you are wet
> As rain itself
> The blood on the wings of that dove
> Gone to hide in a field of leeks
> Form and yet no form
> The crime of pure happiness which needs only to be unveiled
> Cut the inner facet of the marble

Iris/   stripes incarnadine/   autumn/   Alice
Liddel!

"My Approaches to Alice"

Departing from the imagery-oriented and high-velocity poems of the late 1960s and returning once more to the dry, hard language of his earlier poems (and thereby recovering sense, if only to a limited extent), Yoshioka now offers a still new type of poetry to the reader. Evidently, the experiment with language which he has been pursuing has reached maturity, and the result is the ever involved syntax woven into complex layers of images resembling diamond needles, and the eroticism which can be surprisingly realistic from time to time. Yoshioka has completely surmounted the futile influence of the Japanese modernist movement of the prewar period. He now elegantly stands on a totally new poetic ground that is his alone.

Yoshioka's poetry owes much to the act of seeing. His eyes, sharp as a bird's and forever shining with curiosity, take nourishment from a wide variety of things—paintings, dances, plays, the swinging breasts of a stripteaser, and so on.

Also, as is increasingly noticeable in *Saffron Gathering* and *Summer Banquet* (pub. 1979), Yoshioka now willingly admits the words of other poets, writers and painters into his own poems. "If only her petals curled up a little more" says one of the opening lines of "My Approaches to Alice", and this quotation from Lewis Carroll proves a happy one, like many others. The adept use of citations in Yoshioka now makes for a very enjoyable kind of poetry, much like Ezra Pound's.

In his own words, Yoshioka has introduced into Japanese poetry "a celebration in darkness which is at once weird and refined, scatological and lofty, comical and serious."

Yoshioka Minoru has many friends, mostly poets and painters, who were born in the 1930s, but relatively few of his own age. Perhaps it is the distinct youthfulness of his poetry that enables this poet to enjoy such a tremendous influence on poets who are still in their twenties. Also a talented book-designer and a very warm person, this elegant poet of stature occupies a place that is unique among the poets now writing in Japanese.

Yoshioka Minoru

Still Life

night comes and inside the hard surface of the vessel
brightness grows
autumn fruit
apples pears grapes and the like
placed upon one another
they all go together along
to sleep
to mellifluence
to magnificent music
at the most recondite place inside each of them
lies the nucleus gently
around which circles
the rich time of decomposition
now in front of the teeth of the dead
mute like stone
all this fruit
grows heavier
within the deep vessel
& behind this mere semblance of night
it sometimes
sharply tilts

Solid

my slant on things discomfits many others   sometimes I apply a razor edge to
each single plant stalk   to discover at the cut end a rosy family   tragically
aborted   thin membraneous men & women   deprived of water & unable to bite
light   faint sounds of coitus   pollen stains walls & bedding   granular &
rough to the touch   that's why children don't run in the world of toy cars
        their place to play is inside the mother's womb   there they slide & glide
        or in the shade of gourd mellons on a trellis   I quit the pastoral surroundings
quickly   things ought to be solid & sit well   that's my opinion   I close
in on an axe standing against something together with a dragonfly's compound eyes
        I allow my whole figure in an undershirt to be reflected   shouldering a tier of
rainbows & the icicle gimlets from the mountains   I quite dislike all flabby
frogs   solid wings & solid raindrops I caress with both my hands   let me
kick a bottle   just to see how ecstatic I am   it's unbelievable   I hit a
town   beat on the walls of a temple under attack   ah such an excellent game
this   I dog the footsteps of a young woman with child on her way to a hospital
        going uphill   the paving stones begin to convolute & taper   narrower &
        narrower
to a tiny   apex   slippery & white like a belly   time for doctors to laugh
        the evening hours when fire alarms are struck furiously   forceps & scissors
        move
& stretch skin   to pave the way for the head in a bag   the circumference of a
tepid dandelion going to seeds is sharply plucked   fat blows against my undershirt

I panic at the sight of a true solid   overlook & let go unchallenged a coarse
blooded irresponsible army   marching through the tubes inside the fragile body
underneath   enough & I quit the town   wind transforms me into a person
      frozen
      a thing that slides   that's why I never laugh   or say goodby

Octopus

calling across fire
the loving octopus mother gropes among seaweed
hangs from a table of coral
face down
into the deeply religious orifice of the barnacle
prepared to send clusters of phosphorescent eggs
should a captain's corpse
lie sensuously hard by
she strikes eight
& only then
does the octopus mother like a bewildered lover
hug the moving rock

the reproduction of octopuses displays a cursed form   it closely resembles
flesh scattering like a paper umbrella wet & torn   the male octopus's seven
legs hug water into themselves   the one remaining leg that tapers at its far
end functions as a tubular organ   at a glance it seems no more than a shoe lace
       searches for the female's tiny hole   can this be called coitus   water
       undulates
       in a world where things are transparent there is no joy & ejaculation is quick
       close by are the female's widely opened eyes   a touch of pantheistic malice in
them   pregnant now she goes back to her stone nest at the bottom of the sea
       lays two hundred thousand transparent eggs   & braving starvation   onto the
bagful of eggs bunched like grapes   frantically keeps blowing foam   to provide

needed oxygen   in the shade of the wavering seaweed   after this one single
ovulation she turns into a lump of putrefying flesh

just as woman is begotten of wretched imagination
from salt & water the octopus appears
a jet black abstraction painting
sand is buried in sand
a shellfish lives inside itself
maybe that is something now gone by
a woman comes swimming from far off the summer's shore

Comedy

in a kitchen corner   an egg with its back split open becomes visible   near
the long night's shore   a man who has been sleeping stands up   he carries
on his shoulder a cat wearing a hat   the man digs a hole for his dying wife
     exit a hand cart laden with food & money   its way is hindered by the legs of a
bed & by other furniture   because the man passes his hand over the cat
deploringly   the mouse in the cat's throat melts like a bunch of grapes
     which puts out the moon in the center of the view   forest trees begin to
     change
direction in the distance   soon to be covered with snow   which will bring
the man & the cat into the room   but no need to walk   all the time the man
has been pouring wine into his glass by the fireplace   & the cat scurrying about
in the garret   sensitive to cold the man has an eye on the cat which sheds hair
     the total nudity of the cat dazzles the man & he lowers his eyes   the birds that
look into the night's window   all assume the shape of his dead wife's hair & the
man shoots them down   he calmly disjoints the cat   his skillful wave hand
sinks into a pot of butter which has grown yellower   enthralled by the dangerous
culture   the man puts on a doctor's beard & perspires   without intending to
the cat breaks the glass   at that moment the man must surely be relieved
     because the fingers inside the sprayer stop the acceleration of amoebae   & retro-
gress into a human hand   even shed shiny blood among the broken pieces   no
doubt wanting to hold something heavy   the man looks around   is surprised to
find himself being surrounded by scissors & other pieces of hard furniture   from
then on such uninjured parts   as his legs face & genitals he treats with sudden
great care   out of a well-made skin bag   the man will never again come

Simple

feared by none he died   a man with a very prominent tail bone   his wife hated
him   he had a tongue that glistened rather coldly in comparison with his eyes
    his full-breasted wife just couldn't stand it   sluggish   except when he was
eating   totally to be precise devoid of motion   like a plant   especially
when he went to bed   like those parts of a plant that put forth no flowers
    pulled downward by a spider's thread   until finally flat on the ground   a
dismal posture frankly   but to his dead wife it makes no difference now
    only her wavy hands still daily feed the dog that he keeps behind the walls   it
is this false evidence that keeps his wife from dying with all her heart   the
cat that inherited her good qualities is still on the roof & alive under the snow
    this vexes her   if only she could snake her belly out from behind the dark
    far enough to push it into the room where he still walks around   she would
    stand
a good chance   because then she would be able to conceive a plaster foetus
    the dog is looking after his home life   making him laugh & giving him
    trouble
    but it is not capable of any further luscious operations   the man figures that
in order to keep alive he must bring his dead wife's cat back   from the roof
where only dust is falling   must teach it tricks   not worldly things   but
train it to become say a beautiful woman   warm it in bed the first night
    & raise the moon that is favored by the drowned   so he raised his voice to
impregnate the cat   with naked womanly postures   & the bashfulness of a half-
ripe peach heaving a sigh under the leaves   summer came with its sashes of

lightning undone   is his death a testimony to his human nature?   dog's blood dancing in his head   & cat hair still thick on the lower part of his body   he was taken from the powerful country of sweat   & buried in a goose-flesh cold hamlet in the middle of nowhere

Tenderhearted Firebug

Charlie always wishes he did not have to
trim a bald head in the middle of summer
much less shave a little girl's face
fuzz all around her mouth
so indecent it makes you think of the rainy season
like the belly of a milk-drinking doll
Charlie the barber would like to paw the white scalp
of a refrigerator every day
it's got guts almost ready to go off
like the fine fire engine bell Charlie loves
fish for cats lined up dead
coke bottles tinkling
Charlie wants his water ice cold
& his formless tears frozen
no memory of ever being a little boy
but a record of setting forest fires 14 times
32 year old Charlie
is a screaming photograph of war that will never fade
flying his mother & sister like gulls
over blood
is also a pulley chuting down through a total blackout
if a beard makes the grownup
then Charlie is a grownup pickled in vinegar
the poisonless sardine meat in the barracuda's mouth
if obesity is a sin

then Charlie's body weight is zero
his head is the tail of an American mouse on fire
a ring of fire
spinning round & round
it's something more metaphysical than electricity
Charlie's imprecating heart like a skinned rabbit
juts out from other people's thick-coated humanity
it's a painting in paroxysm
not an infection in cold contempt
of the general public but a general infection
the red of yellow wax closed
to other people's prying
Charlie's escape drama
see Charlie in flight
from one iron pole to another
from the American upper air stream
to the india ink China sea of torn sharks?
other people's hearts are not hot enough to ignite a match
but even today even this afternoon
tenderhearted firebug Charlie Colden
drools hot saliva
real forests are all lonely beds that produce fire
cigarette filter celluloid box
Charlie's tools are all very small
they transform everybody's mundane ordinariness
into an extraordinary octave
junk art
is this a victory of Charlie's anti-commercialism
from other people's balcony in South Canyon
a comforting pillar of flames can be seen in the distance at night
Charlie refuses to run away
he will on the contrary visit
or on the contrary he will stand still

the weak eyes of a cicada perched on a rock
forbid seeing
the black branched joys of living
the beautiful way of death
practiced by milkmaids & birds
the bridal dress beyond the trailing smoke
a fire in his head Charlie is
putting out the burning wings   the fire of self
"the rain gear   don't forget your rain gear"
        "the rain gear   don't forget your rain gear"
tenderhearted Charlie Colden
discharges into a tortoise shell
till the rainy season nears

Legend

a chair   jumping down from the chair   a cat   close shot of its feet naked
in its hair   for a fraction of a second   then gone   sucked into the deep
folds of a flower   everybody is surprised nothing like this before   four legs
of wood   limp across the floor for a second   come to a sudden   halt in a
corner of the room   the chair becomes legend   a man   he knows nothing
about the incident   comes out from under the blanket   sets himself in the
chair   letting out circulating heat & stench   assiduously he pulls out the
tube in his anus   starts to grow in bulk   uncontainable rubber   occupies
the whole room   writhes   everything pulsates   pleasure expands contracts
      nighttime now   the man's face the cat's face   side by side in the coil of the
tube   a long time   darkness grows   the man suppresses his breathing   on
the point of extinction he cries   Fire

44

Horse: A Picture of Spring

at that moment I'm lying on race track grass   watching a deformed globular
    squatting horse
      I've seen it prance once or twice!   if it were true that there is a dead horse
in the cupboard of my house   how that would delight me   at once I would
cherish the sponge that was the horse's buttocks   far into the night   looking
back on my life without vacillation   I would make up my mind to protect all
minority rights   a liquor bottle & a blood soaked driving wheel would come
tumbling out of the cupboard   at the end I would measure the girth of an iron
cylinder full of holes   the horse's head would change its elasticity when water
beat down on it   that to me would be the affected part in the heart of the old
warpaths   my surprise at finding it has the same thickness as the woman's neck
    under a star half crunched away like an apple   I would bask in the pity of all
my neighbors   out of a darkness more impermanent than torn canvas   I press
my mouth   to the paunch of the horse I caress   & whisper "human happiness is
innate in each individual"   the woman puts on a skirt over her hooves
    & will go back to the bushy road full of gentle curves both pink & grey   I
    can't
ask anybody   whether the woman is a dead horse   or the deformed globular
    squatting horse that I
once saw in the light   & that is still prancing in the rain   looks like morning
has come   ah such amazing fruit from the date tree   I will brush my teeth
    & the brush will slip out of my hand   the world always makes a surplus of
    things
    & gives me extra work to do

Sentimentality

I

pull down the steel shutters
no commonplace habits mine
even my mind is steel-clad
I'm a man hiding in a box
seen & remembered by a plumber who just happens to be passing by
the girl who laughs at me
as I squat in the toilet
is eating a peach with her back turned
she hates the hammer of the plumber who has his hat pulled well over his eyes
because he would not let her use the water to wash her peach
& caused the narrow source of honey to run dry
the girl who is still in her young-bag days
still ignorant of a grownup woman's summer of sweat
will someday come running too
into my box house
will hug the deformed pillar at the entrance to the law office out front
until then temporarily closed
let a giraffe run all the way down from the roof to the bed
& paint the whole place
already it's as dark in here as a cathedral

II

a lotus opens on the water in a goldfish bowl
the beginning of a bad season
the girl is changing beneath thin skin
begins to transfer black juice from the crown of a flowering plant
into an opaque lobster-shaped bag
it is then that birds fly through the rain-wet bush in my nostrils
all the narrow necked bottles
on the shelf in the darkness
begin to itch & quiver
what change am I waiting for
what exchange

III

the sliced surface of my sleep becomes smooth as agate
the one woman who happened to be there
a handsome-limbed woman in deceptive widow's weeds has been with me since
     yesterday
underneath my magnanimous carnal desire now
as a composition of leg lines
the upper half of her body has been at my service since morning
especially the nebula of pretty freckles behind the shoulders
terribly captivates my mind
at moments enlightens
I presume she has committed a murder
if not her sickly husband
then the gallant who can easily shoulder a bag full of potatoes

if not a man then something else
a big-headed salamander perhaps must have been the victim

IV

experience leads me to betray the accused
it is in the nature of the accused that the accused can't be saved
they all make statements well worthy of punishment
for example I'm brought into a court of justice that is merely props
& am surrounded as accused by people in black
     "my wife is that which is sold to the ant world
     & melts   a shining naked bag of sugar" I blurt out
I make an unfavorable impression
& go to jail my shoulders those of a criminal
my lawyer hurries back to his wife kids & parents
his buttocks full of grains his neck the fatted neck of a chicken he goes out
         into the rain
the unfortunate are fed wire & inhabit a dark place

V

the woman's husband is an expert seaport engineer
every day he goes to the sea with a welder
from working long months & years under the sea
the welder when daylight hits him walks crab-fashion
all the hairs on his body shine
bubbles all over the place
bubbles bitter & very sticky
the husband just builds a fire on the shore
a woman pops up
from between a wrecked ship & a broken net
that is to say the engineer's wife brings food & takes a swim
the floor of hot sand changes the human mind into a complicated conch
& sets cold fish jumping about at the same time

the three people's meal after that is dangerous
dishes & forks move dismally
meat & eggs are all consumed without a trace
vegetables are bashfully left over
the sea is filled with dead men

VI

I look again into the lotus flower
no conversion there
none of the cords around the women of the world is undone
frogs too are squeezed tight
I dream of blond hair blown out from the deepest recesses of the flower
I reach my hand to the woman's thigh
in order to save myself & the unfortunate woman
mourning dresses are of a color & a shape very difficult to distinguish from night
besides they slip off when the time comes
after that I am a faithful game keeper
make up my mind to raise the chicks found in the grass
I hear the woman's voice now changed to that of a water-hen wading near the shore
in a shack safely away from all laws & smog
well protected from all vulgar foods
I lay siege to a beautiful castle of teeth all alone
& win all the other beautiful spoils
the setting sun is that which shines
& sobs
a waterfall hangs from the woman's hair & freezes
calmly I read the golden syntax of the Code
let's see now I think I have served the woman pretty well
let the sinful woman go then
long shall I wait now for the peach-girl to arrive with a child who looks like
        the plumber & press me for marriage

Spindle Form I

mother has a crook in her neck   female nonetheless   father is a small man
with invisible bones   male   in the vacant lot outside the window people
    unable to die pile
up bottles with their mangy hands   flies swarm around them   loud hollow
laughter & tearful voices   they give the couple time to go to bed together
    when night puts on sharp horns   the others will sink beneath the *tatami*
    fire soaked in blood   spreads into mother's womb   father a slimy
    monkey
now hangs from the branch of his self & shrieks   water water   mother a
monster cauldron bottom joined to a broom   she enters the world of sliding
doors   from early morning father keeps his hoe-like hands immersed in a pail
    strikes the hot iron that will stand the strain of labor   his notched file
sharpens ten thousand gimlets   all run through the melancholy *tatami*   that
is his living   is money   father lays down the long long belly of his
bellows   mother is getting big behind the paper doors

Spindle Form II

alive now   I touch   long held down   months & years beneath love & the
waters   an egg inside a small bag   sleeping horizontally   getting up I
bite my toe nails   my piety begins to grow then   mornings & evenings I
listen to maternity's sweet retches   every meal time is a solid time
     perhaps I'll be able to stand up   how small the cathedral I'm in   naked
     no   less than naked   I'm a candle casting my own shadow on the walls
     right left in front & back   no dog this   nor bird   no gift of wings
     sweet dream model come true of appelation father & appelation mother
     an extraction summoned to live   passing through an arch soaked in the
     blood of
drugged & aromatic night   april   somebody's hopechest is opened   in this
capital made of wood
     an old woman in floss silk performs her ablutions

Diarrhea

I have diarrhea   not that I wanted it   just couldn't help it   night
comes & the change of times laps over personal work & I have diarrhea   the
water in the basement   where the phlegm that lends color to crimson flowers
& the twilight sky is spat   is it a phenomenon peculiar to me I wonder
    I have diarrhea today & I had diarrhea yesterday   I think all of us have it
every day   as we look inside the green squashes of our old memory   all the
world's toilet bowls are brought together freshly washed   my diarrhea washes
down my mind   & is communicated to the minds of others   it goes on to
    taint
the food for the starved masses   throngs of men & women of all ages lie idly
around from that moment on   their modest voices   the pathetic movement of
their limbs   they excrete love as proof of being alive   everybody is in a
driftwood position   I myself am a little above them   & am showered with
ashes   I take masochistic meals & have ludicrous metaphysical diarrhea
    probably foreign to horses & dogs   conducted by the pain that comes albeit
feebly from my being alive   I come to witness a soaring construct in that
space   where thunder ends all strife   the flow of a martyr's blood in my
mortal body gurgles & I have diarrhea   I lacerate my entrails   on sloping
ground to be cultivated   & underneath rocks where springs to be drawn will
never run dry   & the civil war of my heart is averted for good   I am
forgotten   I forget things & people   friendships made in hypothetical
situations all   a phenomenal darkness   no longer crouched in the ugly
hypnosis of diarrhoeic modernity frozen stiff   changes its dimension in the

52

garden of the twentieth century   in the center of which natural light comes
into contact repeatedly   I achieve totality as a man in good health   & begin
by eating a pear   here starts a new relationship   a dialogue

Monks

I

four monks
lounge about in the garden
sometimes they assume the shape
of sticks on which black cloth is rolled
without hatred
they flog a young woman
until bats shriek
one prepares the meal
another goes out in search of sinners
a third abuses himself
a fourth gets himself killed by a woman

II

four monks
each devoting himself to service
bringing down the holy figurine
hoisting a cow onto the cross
one shaves the head of another
the dead one prays
still another makes a coffin
just then a flood of childbirths come surging in from the midnight village
in unison the four of them get to their feet
four disabled umbrellas

beautiful walls & linings on the ceiling
a hole appears there
& rain begins to fall

III

four monks
come to the table for supper
the one with long arms deals out the forks
the one with warts pours out wine
the other two don't show their hands
but touching today's cat
& future's woman
their hands mold a thickly haired image
in which are embodied both woman and cat
flesh is that which fastens bones
flesh is that which is washed in blood
two of them grow fat from eating
the other two lose flesh from making

IV

four monks
go out for morning penance
one in the shape of a bird goes to the wood to welcome a hunter
another in the shape of a fish to the river to peep at the maid-servants' crotches
a third comes back from town as a horse carrying a load of weapons
a fourth sounds the bell because he is dead
never do the four burst out laughing in unison

V

four monks
plant seeds in the fields

by mistake one of them dedicates
a turnip to the buttocks of a child
the mouth of its astonished mother whose face is ceramic
sinks a sun of red mud
three of the monks are singing in chorus
on a very high trapeze
the dead one
tries his voice inside the throat of a nesting crow

VI

four monks
lean over a well
goats' scrotums to wash
too many menstruation belts to wash
three of them join efforts to wring
a sheet the size of a balloon
the dead one carries it on his shoulder
& dries it on the tower in the rain

VII

four monks
one of them writes the origin of the temple & the histories of the four
another writes the lives of the world's flower queens
a third writes the histories of the axe & the chariot & the monkey
a fourth because he is dead
hides himself from the others & burns one after another
the histories that the other three write

VIII

four monks
one causes the births of a thousand love children in the land of withered trees

a second lets a thousand love children die in a sea devoid of salt & the moon
a third is surprised to find that a thousand pairs of dead feet & a thousand
            pairs of live eyes weigh exactly the same
on the scale where a snake & grapes are entwined
a fourth though dead is still ill
coughing on the other side of the walls

IX

four monks
abandon the fortress of breastplates
with no life-long fruit of labor to gather
they hang themselves & sneer together
on a place one step higher than the world
and so
the bones of the four retain the thickness of the winter trees
& stay dead till the age comes that will break the ropes

Saffron Gathering

on a palace wall somewhere in Crete
there is said to be a magnificent fresco
"The Gathering of Saffron"
there   a boy on all fours
gathers saffron
among the rocks the sapphire waves repeating convoluted patterns day after day
but were sun to shine on the boy's forehead
though we only see him from behind
salt shaped like stars would surface
when on a promontory in evening the boy's cleft buttocks
thrust out we
recognize the trickle of fragrant sap from a stalk of saffron
waves come   white chopped waves
next the decapitated
beautiful neck of a monkey is displayed
atop the quartz-like cavernously dark
face of the boy whose eyes are shut
like an Arcinboldo portrait
composed of spring fruit & fish
everything putrefies
from the surface
the torso of the monkey
tanned by the faith & curses beneath the Aegean
in the night that even virgin skin cannot resist
the dead blue hair that quivers

what do the boy's shoulders support
is it his nurse's thighs
is it the concealed phallus of the monkey
in the mirror it is reflected
like a hieroglyph
the evening glow of sun colors the distant columns first
waves vanish
going round & round inside a brown conch
"Song" is born
pale purple of saffron flowers
were somebody to beckon to him
the boy will run down the ledge
& choose of all forms of temporary death to drown
as for us   for the time being we   will not tell
should not tell
that old wives' tale about a swimming monkey
until the day when the waves wash over the dome of heaven

Still-Born

I

on a large bib lies a still-born child
nobody's enemy
friend to none
a ghost to perpetuate the lineage of the eternally young
or if humanity exists a crown of thorns on humanity's cursed memory
the stench of the eternal mind cum flesh
the fruit of a handsome soul's sweat
once graven in the mother's mirror & womb
a new arrangement of teeth within the earth's gyre
to be dispossessed by none
at work with the father & straddled in straw
solid buttocks inside honest gravity
but from this day on
no apple of the father's false eye
nor the mother's tiger fondling
no brother to little ones the still-born child
a new personage
in the temple of bunched bacteria
for whom the bell of this freezing century has tolled
sheer terror's tribute
judge judged & onlooker
the film of magnificent identity gyrates
not in the coffin in flames

is the still-born child
nor under the stars of burial clay
but on that side from which it can watch us

II

in another country of nothing but withered trees
the mother washes the body of her still-born child
from a cruel medieval king comes the order
build a palace from all the bones
this servitude of fire done
still-born children go
in flocks & packed inside horses' hooves
away from the land that was raised with the mothers' tears
midday is the torture time favored by the king's men
one mother given to each withered tree
more withered trees & more mothers to hang
a million withered trees sway & a million mothers are torn
a cliff of wombs hangs from an August sky
with fierce eyes the world's mothers see
                                   a forest fire

                   hear at the same time
        the cataclysm come to quench the fire

III

the still-born child discovers by chance
that all the beds in the world creak
each politely bearing one old person
out of numberless loose faucets belly worms come
abandoning the old & death
they head in the direction
where busy stomachs are divined
all packed with meat & vegetables
guns are picked up & aimed here & there

shrieks are heard
wishing cleansed happiness to the old
take the blood slowly to the mountain top
& splash it from there on the beds
of those lovers so firmly married to convention
the only thing the still-born child deplores
is that he is not possessed of sex
he is motified as a belly worm
no early morning fornication for him
no soft bed of silk for the still-born child
no cool intimate place in the shade of the wheat field
but the darkness of the mother's mourning dress
to repeat his solitary orgy in
his passionate buddings of stone
forbidden procreation   castrated glory
then learn if possible the science of extinction
it is the season of forest trodden under green satin slippers
the fountain of castration glitters
pumpkins bloom fully
the still-born child shares his bed with all the dead old men of the world

IV

as to the development of the still-born child & his illness
all the doctors keep silent
the rampage of a beast that causes the source of honey & sponge to run dry
no mother's breasts to be seen on any horizon
all cloaked under bad weather & violence
prying can only find
sulfuric acid crystalized
thus the times go astray among the rocks of sorcery
the arithmetic of foxy merchants who send too much autumn fruit
down the river brings about illness

nails don't grow outward on still-born children
but inward to where dreams are conceived
the still-born child's disease
gets worse & worse in direct proportion to
food & the father's timidity
& finally disappears in a dense fog of powder smoke
the still-born child is remembered in no clinical records
but by cemetery violets feeding on historians

V

dead child on her back a mother goes on pilgrimage
in the capital of a world of wax

    a general of moles torn to pieces
    a night camp in the coils of headless horses' intestines
    a violated girl burned roofs visible between her thin thighs
    fish marrying a soldier killed in a marsh in the morning
    men-of-war in spiderweb turrets all sinking
    under the sea chiseled out by the teeth & nails of a coal stoker

a still-born child's favorite spectacles all
but the mother's love is quick
take the tragic toys away from the dead child
train him properly
punish him when disobedient
expose his private parts before ladies & gentlemen at table in broad daylight
from the height where the coats of arms of all the nations in favor of
    night-operations are ripped to pieces
hang the dead child's hair
flourish his hairless slippery head
put him to shame
throw light on the physical humiliations of the father & his brethren
& on the melancholy roses of those men's souls

until pain makes the dead child incontinent
the yellow dead child of a broom
the dead child of marble
the black dead child of iron wire
the dead child of a blond forest the numerous dead children of sand
meanwhile
in a land where trees shelter summer cicadas
a wise mother her voice still tearful but different
makes by means of a different kind of energy
an identical history of anger

VI

the favorite pastime of still-born children
is to team up
& throw a net into the coral sea
cause the heavy testicles of the men who sank with canons to resonate
decorate colorfully women's anuses sucking in sand & darkness
relish perfect peace of mind when working for the dead
break the shackles of salt & iron
patch up the bodies with strong glue
make them serviceable again this time in the land of withered trees
golden fish scales jingle silver fish scales ring
enraptured days with sharks' teeth biting
peaceful bones find the bed service of sea water boring
still-born children can hear them say that
then let's spread the net again from the moon as wide as possible
collect anything that is dead
the mother makes grimaces & won't give a hand
she shouts in her house a wrecked ship
you can't exchange dead things for nothing
the still-born child's voice is too small to insist
he hides himself from the mother's eyes
& lies down on his side quite frozen

& by his side lies the sea
the sea where legend can be traced

VII

when the mother has gone to sleep
the still-born child crawls about on the floor
in the end more still-born children will rise
& fill the sea under a spring storm
faces all upturned as befits the dead
they go jumping about one after another
in search of their violated sister
not just one sister but sisters without number
beckoned by the spirit of the waves
holding funereal flowers over their heads
they go to the sea where blood is mixed & dishonored
& cleanse the pillars of thighs
sisters conceive & sisters bear
innumerable still-born children for a midnight celebration
a royal road the still-born child will open
into a primeval virgin land
& there he will see
the future delivery scene
the maternal lightning torn open
& from that immense bloody darkness out will come
white-haired still-born children one after the other

VIII

mothers arrive each with a dead child
from a certain hemisphere a certain deserted capital
in liveries of mourning dresses all draggle-tailed
a few even with a dog of penitence
they go into the desert until it is filled to capacity
other chattering mothers now forced into silence

move from the village to the seashore
the religious flow of black sashes without a break
lest the dead children should come alive again
humor them with nursery songs & nightmares
& establish dominion throughout this mundane world
how could flesh & blood sing the death of this civilization
together in thunderous chorus
last of all half the widowed mothers line the glacier
see those voluptuous hips
each slapping her child on the buttocks
as proof of possessing a dead child each
& just as the child cries out in pain
this long & difficult night journey of vengeance will end
above the world of mourning dresses
the tip of a pyramid is seen
only when gathered thus without number
will the mothers be able to start a new sky
inside their furious hair
& a constellation of real numbers be laid

Family Photograph

mother wears a traditional underskirt
along the *tamo* tree the hanging tree
the sun rises
in the graveyard of the island
a fierce man eats a hundred thrushes
such is the dark mind of a father full of obligation
o no not again
big sister
still hides the rugby ball
that came rolling from the park
& so the cat who is our lodger
soaked in the rain that runs on the surface of the marsh
like a goblin
little sister is
on a goodwill trip night after star-shiny night
is everybody there now
then we'll take our picture
give us a big smile
face up to the sky
but will we have a good picture I wonder
already I am
in the back country near the Mediterranean
growing up with a cork tree

In Praise of the Old and Senile

an old man   a cheerless naked child and a pelican
                              trailing along after him
establishes
                    against the day when he will die
                    king
                    of the afflicted
the moral character of flesh/the insularity of mind
saws a whole wood and builds   ever so slowly
          a phantom ship
          underneath his night clothes
                    nothing
                    but broken teeth
                    on board
sails forth from his native land farewell
          to piles and lung troubles
rides the deep waves of his skin
turns his hairy wife over wrong side up
               wits are scattered
               jelly fish not seen through
               in the pitch dark
               poison from her breasts
the old man laughs
and laughs   hurrah   banzai   death
          a new experience
                    at least this once

come night cross the frontier it's off the hinges
   rupture proof fish's belly sheds light
   without a break shrinks without a break builds up a terrible
   pressure is erotic won't let the old
   man of decorum go
   to sleep
the old man recollects
       so bewitching
       the moon
       of antiseptic gauze
rather he creates
   all for his own stomach and bladder naturally
hyena howling vulture shrieking desert nights
& cities of stars and equally of sands
& he sits in the middle of a flame inside a shack
   unable
   to excite
   the extravagant blood
   vesseled in a king's heart
     useless
   like a bamboo basket
       left on its face and useless
his is an uneasy world of hair
       no gorgeous naked dancer there
a barber's razor flashes & shaves his big pate
      that cold plaster touch
then moved
the old man
   dead now and therefore beautiful
   a tutelary god
       of kids and pelicans
moved to where he is in nobody's way

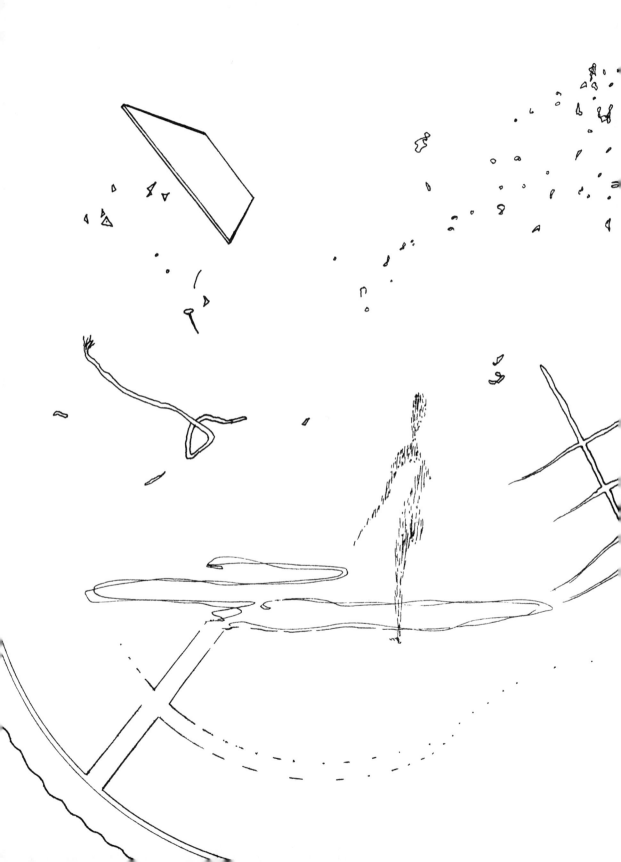

Strangers' Sky
Iijima Kōichi

Strangers' Sky

The birds are back
Pecking the black void of the earth.
Circling up, down
Round the now alien roof-top.
Lost . . . ?

The sky buries its head in its hands
As if it had eaten stones.
Broods.
Blood it cannot bleed veins the air
Like a stranger, circling.

Iijima Kōichi— "Strangers' Sky. . . ."

by Tsuruoka Yoshihisa

Iijima Kōichi was born on February 25th, 1930. His boyhood was deeply affected by the war. When on December 8th, 1941, Japan started the war with a surprise attack on Pearl Harbor, Iijima was in the third year of high school (under the old system) and he joined those mobilized to work in a shipyard producing parts for special-purpose submarines. In 1945 he took and passed the examination to enter the Military Flying Academy, but in August of the same year Japan lost the war. Iijima returned to his native Okayama, then in ruins after enemy air-raids, to resume his high school life there. The awakening and establishment of his self-identity thus took place in the midst of wartime disorder.

Iijima started writing poems in earnest around 1946 (he was reading Baudelaire and Supervielle then), and the first collection of his poems entitled *Strangers' Sky* came out in 1953. The war still is strongly felt in this volume, written during the last years of his adolescence. The fireweeds growing among the ruins excite fellow-feeling in him, but he is skeptical about the energetic reconstruction that soon starts all over Japan. Superficial and statistical prosperity does not inspire him. ". . . I only have words to cope with this. I can only build cities with words. That is the reason for my poetry" — Iijima is to write later looking back on his first years as a poet. What to seek is "total freedom", through words, in contradistinction to the "false" prosperity and freedom that have replaced fascism.

> Soon we shall learn to recognize a sound.
> In that small sound when a vessel touches another.
> In that sound when a wind walks away.
> In that sound when an oar cleaves the water.
> In that sound inside our selves.
>
> Look in it for a road.
> Look in it for a woman's face.
> The roads are without number.
> But we shall choose one and no other.
>
> "Road"

This poem from *Strangers' Sky* clearly defines Iijima's stance toward the world around him. Just as the decision to start the war was made by others in his ignorance, postwar Japan almost totally alienates him. What his mind still recalls is that sky and that sun above those ruins of 1945, and he listens eagerly for a small sound there in order to discover a new "road". His poetry reveals this search for that "road".

In 1955 Iijima encountered surrealism, and the next year he joined other contemporary poets (Ōoka Makoto among others) to form a surrealism society. He personally knew Takiguchi Shūzō (a prominent Japanese surrealist who had been active from before the war and in direct contact with André Breton), which perhaps bore a part in bringing him to surrealism. Iijima's yearning after that white-heated summer sun in the face of postwar realities linked itself directly to surrealism which sought to liberate living and thinking totally from all containment. *Five Poems At An Hour Before Dawn and Other Poems* (pub. 1967) is the result of the above union.

> Infinitesimal roses

> Infinitesimal sand
> Infinitesimal impossibilities
> Infinitesimal stalks
> Will there be an infiltration
> Of those things
> Into other infinitesimal
> Roses, sand, impossibilities, stalks. . .?

In this collection we constantly meet a consciousness attempting to keep itself at a distance by means of automatic writing. Here words acquire the hardness of things so as to break themselves of the traditional lyricism of Japanese poetry (*tanka* and *haiku*). Difficult as it must have been, Iijima's surrealist technique has enabled him to effect this separation from lyricism. What is more, even humor begins to appear in his poetry now:

> . . .
> In my already funereal dominion
> Erect
> One
> Pure
> Transparent city.

To build a "transparent city" is just what *An Esquisse on the Private Ownership System* (pub. 1970) does with its perfect language. With Iijima "seeing" is always equated to the restoration of hope, and this logic further develops into the art of "seeing the invisible." The volume harvests a series of poems entitled "The Visible" which begins as follows:

> The geographies I pursued alone in my dreams
> Must be committed to paper. . .

If attaching importance to dreams is equivalent to contemplating the invisible, keeping accounts of those dreams will be comparable to forcing the invisible to materialize on paper.

> . . .
> A sea urchin moves
> A sea urchin moves
> A volcano exists
> For a split second a volcano   rocks
> Across a camp dripping with sweat
> A volcano moves
> A volcano moves
> Misery moves
> Misery exists
> Or it does not. . .

The mushy red substance inside a sea urchin exists, and is visible, just like the lava, the undulating magma, inside a live volcano. The visible and the invisible are linked here, or, in other words, reality and dreams correspond. Such is the world presented by Iijima's poetry. And if a volcano "moves" so does misery. Here nature (volcano) and human existence (misery) are both defined as visible. In this manner Iijima's poetry focuses on the visible as a synthesis of reality and non-reality. At this subtle junction of reality and nonreality Iijima keeps spinning his poems, carefully avoiding clear-cut conclusions: each of his poems is at once a testimony to hope and an act of fate.

    Goya's First Name? (1974), *Barcelona* (1976), *Miyako* (1979), *Wander Up and Down In Ueno and Penetrate Ōu* (1980)—Iijima has been publishing substantial volumes one after another. In the first two books mentioned above the main theme is the poet's trip to Spain. Miyako, Ueno, and Ōu are all place names; in the latter two books as well travel constitutes the main subject. The "walking" or "moving" rhythm has always been the bottom current in all of Iijima's poems ever since *Strangers' Sky*: his attitude toward reality and dreams seems to be furnished with this rhythm as its basic, built-in mechanism. In all of the four books above that have come out of his mature years Iijima is always spurred by a sort of wanderlust, an impulse to start on a journey which is another form of "walking." Perhaps to be on the move serves the practical purpose of shoving him out of his occasional mental depressions, besides offering him new aspects of reality.

> The memory of walking   persists
> Inside my body.
> Whom am I to tell
> About this walking in my dreams?
>
> The memory of something that can never be told in words
> This body keeps
> But in what depth?
> Such a consciousness is   perhaps   time.
>
>   "The Memory of Walking"

The journeys that Iijima makes are but instances of "this walking in (his) dreams." When he writes poems he is attempting to say the unsayable, performing an act of exorcism for the well-being of his body and mind. Somewhere in the notes attached to *Miyako*, Iijima tells us that in Okinawa a magical formula ("*ishigandō*") is often inscribed on stone walls for the purpose of charming away evil spirits. Perhaps Iijima's poems, too, are each of them "*ishigandō*."

Iijima has published a large number of essays on a variety of subjects—French as well as Japanese men of letters, surrealism, art, cinema and so on. He has recently started writing novels as well. We certainly have much to look forward to from this so richly gifted poet.

Iijima Kōichi

America Symphony

Where we were "mobilized for labor" we used to sit
On our heels in a dug-out shelter. We listened to Jazz.
For the first time. From a wretched portable radio
Outlandish melodies came *gatagata*.
Up above a shiny silver speck — a B29 — went *kiin*
The sky was a perfect blue: we saw
That speck purely as object.

The object showered us with incendiaries & machine gun bullets.
That was the end of our war & the end too of
Boiled barley with rice reeking of Bakelite.
The object came down at Atsugi
&from it trooped out lots of GIs.
The object spat out human beings.
The human beings that came out of the object were
Gay goodhearted Yankees.
We read "A Farewell to Arms" for the first time:
Savoring that title so good to our ears.
Popeye ate spinach as before.
In the films the object also spat out
America was busy eating walking & loving.

Fifteen years since then has seen much happen
Between us & America. Now we can
Easily picture the sergeants & sergeant majors

Not much different from us—human beings—
On board the flying objects
Okinawa——Pearl Harbor——Guadalcanal——bloody
Place names still fastened
Between us & America
But with rusted pins now.
Handbills shouting "American Imperialists Go Home"
Were washed & scrubbed away—
Bygones now.
The muddy rivulet beneath Sukiyabashi Bridge was filled in:
No more US marines to be thrown in there in the middle of winter.
All the same—objects still squeak across the sky, still
Turning the Braun tube images on our TV screens into waves
&giving us nerves. How hot how much rain & how noisy the cicadas
In the summer of that surrender year—now gone clean out of our minds.
But I still clearly remember
Hurried footsteps up & down the stairs,
Whispering
&light suddenly flooding our rooms
Finally freed from blackout curtains.
How the sea of sunflowers looked like moonlight.
Father came back from a remote mining town
Carrying a beggar's bag on his back, looking black
&exhausted like everybody else. In time he smiled
As if driven to the end of all his wits.
What was I thinking then? About my poor self completely deprived
Of all sense of balance by an aviation-aptitude testing machine?
About the dusty white narrow rows of houses of Kyoto & their low eaves?
Or about the wormwood colored Korean factory boys
Standing in groups in front of an empty warehouse?
The war that ended like a kite whose string suddenly snaps—

84

Where had it been blown away to now? What was to happen now?
America, that's how lost we were the day you won the war.

Now your Eisenhower is to pay a visit to Japan to celebrate
The centennial of Japan & US friendship. Shall we
Greet the flying object when it lands at Haneda with stars
&stripes in our left hands & little rising suns in our right?
The Japanese government will give the biggest feast ever.
Most of the Japanese people will just watch—with no
Profundity of emotion their eyes will simply recognize
The brave enemy general of the Second World War.
We too will watch. In the rising dust
Our protesting fists will blur.
To act
Has always been someone else's business.
Always someone else's.
Diapers & nylons hang on clotheslines—again today
The murky duralumin sea glitters beyond.
The sea of objects.

Obstinate Anxiety

Today   at a market butcher's
While watching a mincing machine
I got sick
Sweat oozed from me
Breathing became difficult
What was being ground there
Was it not what little we have
In our own empty insides?
Not that we have such a lot of
Insides to speak of or to protect
It was as if
An electrician   or a plumber
Naked from the waist up
Dripping with sweat
Suddenly walked
Into your home
What was it that was being
Exposed there
A faint   but obstinate anxiety
Pestered me all the way home
still   continues

Streams & Rivers

1

You have no large river
Inside you;
That is the ultimate explanation
Of your sorry plight.

I dare say
Your misery is attributable
To the absence of a large river
Inside you.

2

I saw a river just once
This last summer.
One day at Ohizumi I got on a train
Heading for Seibuchichibu, away from Ikebukuro.
It was still morning.
There were only a few passengers in each car.
Wind came in from open windows.
That was the only time I enjoyed coolness
This last summer.
A river appeared to meander
Among the mountains.
It went on & on without end.
It was an authentic river
Running just for its own sake.
That river

Was the most noble entity
I saw this last summer.

3

That river
Crosses my mind from time to time
These days. Rivers
Have been haunting me.
For a long time I haven't met persons
Who have a river inside,
Much less any
Who have a large river inside.

4

Water
Quenches thirst.
But there is a kind of thirst
That can't be quenched.
That kind of thirst
Exists indomitably
&accompanies you
Everywhere.

5

In the summer of 1945
You were in the town of N to which you had moved for safety.
In the garden of Mr S's main house (there were such things as main houses then)
You were in the company of Mr S & his nurses,
All gathered in front of a radio
As the Emperor decreed surrender.

Everybody was tongue-tied

Only the sky above was shining.
We couldn't bear to look at
Each other's faces.
Unable to either cry or laugh—
As the phrase goes.

Suddenly
Dr S told his wife to go & draw out
All the money from the bank.
Mr S's words at that time
Lingered long
In my ears
As something unpleasant.
But now I think otherwise:
The postwar days of Japan
Started running at full speed
In the direction of Mr S's words.

6

It must have been the 17th or the 18th of that August
I got on a train & went to where the Tenth Foot was quartered
To have a look at the barracks & walk around the walls.
The place looked completely deserted:
No sign of life.
Except on telephone poles and walls by the gate
Those posters that said "All-Out War!"

7

Stations smell.
I have never known anything that had a worse smell
Than the stations in the 20th year of Showa,
Year of the Surrender.
When pushed to the wall

Even beautiful women start smelling like that.

8

I don't remember any more
What I was doing in those days.
I remember the brightness of the river
Only a few minutes walk
From where I lived.

9

One thing was heavy
On my mind.
On August 10th I received a telegram
Telling me to join the Army Aviation Academy
On August 12th.
I figured I no longer had to,
But then I could not ignore the order either, could I?
No need to go now,
But I kind of wanted to go:
My first dilemma after the war.
Thirty years since then
Have found me in similar dilemmas
Without a break.

10

In the summer of 1939
I went with my brother to see the Kinoshita Circus.
Elephants. . .A honky-tonk called "Nature" or something.
The flying trapeze, tight rope walking,
Clowns. . .the big tall tents;
The only things in your country that are a match for cathedrals
Are those tents.

90

When tents were hoisted in a field
We were ecstatic both going and returning.
The smells of animals, the heated atmosphere, the dripping sweat
Crackers, caramels, cold coffee. . .
Above all the smell of those elephants, lions & monkeys. . .
The smell of urine boiled dry by the sun.
(Circuses have no smell
On television)
You were a fourth grader.
Your brother is always a little too wild.
The Kinoshita Circus smacks of the Sino-Japanese War.

11

Television is over summer is over
There is nothing more to think about.
Think then about Mishima Yukio.
In the evening of the day Mishima died on a high veranda
You were meeting a lady
From Nice,
An old lady who is always sprightly
And knows Japan quite well,
In a hotel room at Ohmori,
Well lit but somehow bleak,
She looked tired & dark—the first time I had ever
Seen her tired & somber.
—The way Mishima died, she said
&looked all the more somber.
She showed me some Piccaso woodcuts,
But even Picasso looked gloomy there.
When we were about to part
She gave me a photograph of herself & Picasso
Smiling with their arms around each other's shoulders—
She was much younger in the photo & very proud of it.

You did not like Mishima so much
While he was still alive:
You think a lot about him
Now
That he is gone.

He used to go on television
In a white cambric suit,
And offer us forced martial laughter.
But I'm sure he must have hated television.
He must have found unbearable
This emptiness after television.
I believe I know very well how he must have felt.

He did live in a gorgeous Western-style house,
But that was imitation West;
Even his military uniform was fake.
He was always feeling inferior
To the absolutely genuine élitism
Of the Meiji poet Ohgai.
He put on a fake military uniform,
Waged a fight against all television
& destroyed himself.
(I might respect but would not like at all
Anybody who is incapable of self-destruction.)
He must have wanted to make
Everyday a New Year's Day.
Poor fellow.

But perhaps you like Mishima better
Than anybody else who is involved
In something like literature now.

After Mishima's death

You went mad little by little.
You couldn't bear to look at anyone else's face.

If you hate televion
You cannot survive today.
(Those moments-after-moments when you forced yourself
To learn to watch television)
All Japan is comatose
In front of television sets.

12

Poetry is desperately trying
To keep itself going despite television.
(Desperately is not a word
You like much.)
As you patiently crouch in the virulence of summer
You understand that very well.

13

Thinking of going
To see the river again.
Impossible to think of more
Than that now.
Better
To think of a river
Than to think of blood.
On a train again this windy day,
Windows all closed, stuffy.
Saddened to think there will never be Japanese
"Thought" worthy of the name.
You love now
Only the tragic dead.

Spoon

(On first reading about Auschwitz, January 1961)

One burnt & rusted spoon
Makes the sun's light all the more dazzling
Makes it almost unbearable to see
This spoon
Was once used by a human being to eat food
What he looked like what he was doing
We
Can
Easily surmise
Since we too are human beings
That he found the sun's light
Dazzling
& loved the rustle of the trees
Is certain
But the one that killed him in Auschwitz
What that one was like
We never
Can know
The mind
Boggles
But a spoon
Wrapped in a big worn
Handkerchief

Speaks infinite words
Pulls us all the way back
To that year we thought we had left
Far behind us
January
The sun's light
Is unfurling peace
The trees rustle & sway to the wind

Cut-Out Sky

She has been storing
Aspects of the sky that I have not known.
In her memory
She has several such pieces cut out of the sky.

Sometimes she comes upstairs
&gives them to me
Carefully, one by one.

There is a marsh in the sky,
&it is inhabited
By various creatures, she says.

There is a school child, for example, squatting down
On his heels at a small station built of wood.
She has passed by the station only once,
&the child is carrying a slipper-bag in his hand.

Next she said—
Among pieces of the sky now lost
There have been much clearer ones.

Bokokugo (Native Language)

During the half year I was abroad
I did not feel like writing poems
Even once
I was busy walking around
Oblivious of myself
When asked why I was not writing poems
I never could give a good answer

Now back in Japan
I just have to write poems
Only now am I beginning to understand
That half year
I was busy just walking around
Not writing poems—
It is that I am now back
Into my own *bokokugo*

Inside the word *bokokugo*
Are "mother country" & "language"
During that half year when I was telling myself
That I was cut off from my mother & country & language
I could walk through reality
Immune to harm—

There was hardly any need
For me to write poems

In April Paul Celan
Threw himself into the Seine & died
I believe I can understand that act
Of that poet who was a Jew
Poetry is a sad thing
Poetry is said to put one's national language right
But for me it is not so
Daily I am injured inside my own *bokokugo*
Every night I have to set out
For another *bokokugo*
That is what makes me write poems
Keeps me going

St. Paul de Vence

On top of a hillock in St. Paul de Vence
You are talking now with a lady
About Jacques Prévert
She wanted Prévert
To write good poems
&tried to give him fine Japanese paper
But Prévert said he wrote poems on toilet paper
&declined her offer
Such a wicked person isn't he
But such a fine such an excellent poet
It seems that Jacques Prévert
No longer comes to St. Paul de Vence

Curiously Enough Affinity Grows

Curiously enough, things begin to look alike.
That is a good sign.
As the colors of a forest melt in the rain
As the hot & cool temperatures are shared so readily
By two lovers sitting next to each other
So, little by little, things begin
To flow into one another.
Such a time will come.
It will come
To those who wish for it
With the certainty
Of branches that attract birds.
If it does not come, that is because
It is not beckoned.

Similitude develops.
The color of life,
Enkindled, glows
& similitude grows.
The color of life will not desist.
It blends & thereby attains perfection.
The black of pain & sorrow even will come
To uphold the yellow, red & blue dance of joy.
Affinity increases.

It begins to look like a woman.
A woman
Begins to look like everything else.

In the whirlpool of affinity
The past with its wry face
Loses its pursuer's certificate.
The empty expanse of night
Begins, willy-nilly, to grope for tomorrow's breath.
The world is richer now than before
In the form of one woman
Who, already, is beautiful
Lips, gentle hands & eyes that can
Embrace me, turn me
Face to face with a large deep lake.
Her small throat
Trembles now
Like a bulb that pushes a flower open,
& the sputum that runs over from inside her throat
Flaps its wings, spins light
& becomes tens of thousands of birds.
Next the down-covered hearts of those birds
Go through so many changes to become
Throbbing bulbs.

Curiously enough, kinship spreads.
That is a good sign.
If it does not come, then that is because
It is not beckoned.
Her lake tells me to dream
Of that which is still afar off,
Traps me in its laughter, makes to stop me
From going any farther

& melts my heart which is inclined to be frozen.
We meet on almost fictional streets,
Streets teeming, moreover, with this terrible
Cruelty & gentleness,
Streets extremely hilarious & unhappy
Where din & silence live right next to each other.
Streets where the direct echoes of
The tens of thousands of voices of Budapest & Portside
Slaughtered by 'pirates' & 'gangsters'
Threaten us without a break.
Streets where window cleaners are seen
Pulling themselves up the faces of buildings by their creaking ropes hand over hand.

I agree to believe in one thing.
What more should I believe in?
In order to fill up the long-standing despair,
In order to satisfy the long-standing fiction of our broken hearts,
One night,
One morning
Its clean air
The surprise-attack of a blue sky,
&one encounter fresh & intense
Like gasoline running over,
That's enough.

What Words Are to Us

1

Cheeks dappled by the sun
Our gestures
Still resemble those of refugees.
Hungry eyes become us,
Dry mouth still becomes us well.

Underneath a remote sky
The illusion of an arsenal disintegrates.
The illusion of a future city disintegrates.
The image that becomes visible
On a warping pyrograph.

We are not yet accustomed
To paying our respects to the dead.
We do not catch on to fear.
We are not able to quantify
How much space words will uphold.

Memory associates itself with things unmade;
Words too collect nothing but fragments.
Our field of vision—
A mirror that reflects nothing

Looking out on a plain scattered with dead bugs.

The search to locate a 'place',
A magnetic field where scattering images converge
Is an activity of—the mind?
The line of vision sustained by a hundred refugees—
The constellation of a hundred people.

"The eyes of refugees uphold this century."

2

Words have no flags to hoist.
As we tried to mirror our own selves
On the surface of words
No trembling daybreak sky appeared there;
No flicker of the future city we saw there.

Who crouches
Silently hugging the knees?
The residuum of our ancesters' dreams
Proffered behind the upper arms of people
Or in the depth of their eye-sockets?
Or is it our own peaceful blood?
Are we the ones to arrive last of all?
Or do we stand here before anybody else?
We would be a party to the void,
We would malign those walking now,
If we answered the question without hesitation.

3

An attempt
To etch words on the sky.
On the Tahitian sky   on the sky over a dry land

On the sky above foamy breakers
People have been walking, with burdens on their backs

Trying to catch fish at the water's edge
Using trees for tents. We too
Step into the line. Will the bird's wings flap?
Will springs run over inside people?
Did waterfalls look for entrances?
Our clumsy song begins there,
Crouches there with the severed head of an ox.
It will conduct our own going.
Words that resemble so much the fragments of a cloudy sky.
An attempt to etch words on the sky.

December, 1959

I'd like to write a poem long as a roller bandage, put it round my neck
Cure my influenza. That's the only thing we can do in December
In this metropolis where it's so easy to catch cold.
We who unlike Fascists have no plans to make
What can we do?
Just crowd each other here?
In the year 1886 Berlin, Baden, Koblenz
&Hamburg were also crowded with cabs, & a poet
Who worked as a tutor & was suffering from a heart disease wrote
"We would very much like to be *them*
On the other side of the glass panels of the aquarium.
They dream their dreams right there
Where they were born & right there in their own excrement
They stay put & make love."

At the coffee stand in front a girl in a duster works
Until evening, until her hair is all loose & dry.
She sells a drink that has the same color & taste year in & year out.
Inside the dark building another girl of about the same age
Operates the elevator & she keeps saying
"Third floor, fourth floor" nine to five.
We feel we are their compatriots afflicted with the same trachoma.
I've just come up the stairs from a basement room with people
In wornout overcoats, from an old film in which there were scenes
In a morgue. A man, his name & address unknown, his height

A hundred & seventy-three centimeters, a birthmark
On his face, was lying in a wooden box. He was still unidentified
When he was put in an elevator with an iron railing for a door
& was all very quietly taken to the first floor.

December winds are cold. Our decomposing rhymes too
Are bleak.
Shall we speak up here & call somebody
A few names as loudly as we can?
Will that warm us up?
We too would like to sing beside a redhot burning stove
In our human voice. But we
Cannot sing in our natural voice—we have
Influenza. In order to express ourselves we have to
Dip our pens
In freezing ink.

Shining Circles

I like to go round a prismatic interior like an aquarium
Or to clamber up a tower & then down
And to come back to the old entrance/exit
At exhibitions the world images that you follow crawlingly
Will come full circle
Circuses have their smell, animals & gyrations in the air
In Federico Fellini movies there are tours of the Hell
Purifying caves, secret passages, white plastered woman & the crackle of jesters
I'm always in quest there of the world's vagina, the earth's navel

My ambulations describe a circle which will bring me
Back to the old entrance/exit hundreds & thousands of times
I even opt to run around inside my own nightmares
To be on the move, on the run
To be made sport of by marvel
To be pushed around—
These are doings of my own choosing

Aquariums, exhibitions, circuses & festivals
Everything in our country is no better than a miniature garden
Shivering in poverty-stricken light
No hope for anything electrifying

Like the sparkling bubbles of brass wind boiling over
Even in movie houses people don't laugh much

All the same—in this age of white collars when people are more alienated from
        one another than ever before
I seem to want to go round & round inside shining circles
Like aquariums and towers where rogues, drunks, jesters,
Frenzy, & white-plastered madwomen thrive

Poetry and Catching Catfish

I used to have fun catching catfish   as a child
The other day   I remembered that suddenly
In the darkness of a tunnel   the catfish
Would be hiding
There
The tunnel was a little lower than a grownup's height
Your voice would echo so
Into your net   the fish   would come jumping
A splash   a thump   &a fish in your net
That sensation
Was so alive   in the very navel of your day
(That catfish catching
Was contemporaneous with history
I now know
Say the civil wars   or
The Polish post office incident in Danzig)
Today I   don't catch catfish
But write poems instead
Only   do I
Love the world now
As much as I did then?

The expansion of the world   &the question of one's place in it
Those children so lost in catching catfish
Space-time enveloped them so gently once
The world left them   alone

The Japanese text begins on page 200 and moves in this direction.

歴史と同時進行した
ナマズ捕り）

きょうわたしは　ナマズ捕りのかわりに
詩を　書いている
ただ　あの頃ほど
この世界をわたしは愛しているか
いないか

世界の拡大と　居場所の問題
ナマズ捕りに熱中する子供を
時空はそっとつつんで　いた
世界はかれらを忘れて　やった。

詩とナマズ捕り

子供の頃　ナマズを捕って遊んだことを
このあいだ　ふっと思い出した
ナマズは　川のトンネルの暗いところに
ひそんでいた
そこは
大人の背丈より　いくらか低いトンネルで
声をあげるとよく反響した
手網に　魚は　とびこんできた
パシャッ　ズズズッと　重いナマズが躍り込む
その感触が
一日のまんまんなかに　生きていた
（いま思えば　内乱とか
ダンツィヒのポーランド郵便局事件　とか

115

突き動かされていること
それらをえらぶ

われらの国の水族館も　展覧会も　サーカスも
祭りも　いささか箱庭のようで
貧乏な光線にふるえているようではあるが
万事湧き立つように
金管楽器のきらめく泡の　ふきこぼれるように　とは行かないが
人々は映画館の闇の内部(なか)でさえ　あまり笑わないのだが

それでも他人がますます他人めいてくるこの会社員の時代に
悪党　酔漢　道化　狂乱　白塗りの狂女
それらの栄える　水族館のような　塔のような
輝く円環をぐるぐる歩きすることを求めているらしい。

輝く円環

水族館のようにさまざまの色の動く内部(なか)をまるく一巡して
それとも塔によじのぼって　また下りてき
もとの出口に戻ってくるのが好きだ
世界像をずうっと匂うようにしてへめぐって
また戻ってくる絵画展
サーカスの臭気　動物たち　空中の旋転
フェデリコ・フェリーニの映画の内部(なか)の地獄めぐり
胎内めぐり　抜け穴　白塗りの女たちや道化の嬌声
そこで世界の陰門　大地の中心部がどこか絶えず探している

わたしは円弧を描いて　歩行し
もとの出口に戻る　何百ぺんも　何千ぺんも
わたしは悪夢の中を逃げまわることさええらぶ
動いていること　逃亡しつづけること
驚異に翻弄されること

117

われわれも肉声でうたいたい　しかし
われわれは肉声でうたえないインフルエンザの
われわれを表現するために、
冷えきった
インクにペンをひたすだろう。

同じ年頃の少女は　朝九時から晩五時まで
「三階です　四階です」と云っている。
われわれは彼女らに同じトラホームにかかった
同胞であることを感じる。わたしは
着古した外套の人々といっしょに今
階段をのぼってきた。　地下室でわれわれは
今　モルグの出てくる古いフィルムを見た。
姓名も所番地も不詳の　顔にあざのある
身長一メートル七三センチの男が
木箱のなかに入れられていた。彼は
匿名のまま入口が鉄柵のエレベーターにのせられ
一階にきわめてしずかに運ばれて行った。

十二月の風は寒い。われわれの韻の乱れた
詩篇も寒い。
いっそ他人の悪口をここで二つ三つ
思いっきり怒鳴ろうかそうしたら
少しはあたたかくなるだろうか。
あかあかと燃えるストーブのそばで

119

一九五九年十二月

繃帯のように長い詩を書いて　それを首にまきつけ、
インフルエンザを癒したい　十二月の
この風邪をひきやすい都会でわれわれに
できることと言ったらファシストのように
立案もできないわれわれには
ここでひしめきあっているしかないのか。
一八八六年のベルリン、バーデ、コブレンツ
ハンブルグも辻馬車でいっぱいで、
一人の家庭教師で心臓病の詩人が　《水族館のガラス越しのかれらに
われわれはまったくなってみたい。かれらは生れおちたまさにその場処の汚物のな
かで夢み
そこから動かずに恋愛している》と書いた。

表のコーヒースタンドでは　一人の上っ張りの少女が
年中同じ色　同じ味の飲料を
髪がバサバサにかわく夕方まで売りさばいている。
建物内の暗いエレベーターのハンドルをにぎっている

120

泡立つ波がしらのうえの空に、
人は歩いてきた、荷をにない

水ぎしに獲をもとめて
木々を天幕とした。ぼくらも
その列にはいる。鳥は羽搏くか、
人の身内に泉はこぼれるか
滝は入口をもとめたか。
ぼくらの不器用な歌はそこにまじり、
切られた牛の首とそこにうずくまる。
ぼくら自身の歩みを導く。
曇り空のきれはしによく似たことば。
空にことばを　彫りこむこころみ。

おのれの姿をうつすとき、
そこにふるえる暁の空はうつらず
未来の都市もゆらめかなかった。

ひっそりと膝を組んで
しゃがんでいるのは
人々の眼窩のおく　上膊骨のかげに
差し出されている祖先の
夢の残渣か、ぼくらの静かな血か。

ぼくらは終りに来た者か
はじめに立つ一人か、
口ごもらずに云うことは
虚ろへの加担となろう。
今歩む人への非難になろう。

Ⅲ

空にことばを　　彫りこむ
こころみ。
タヒチの空に　　かわいた地の空に、

122

その計量ができない。

記憶はこわれたものにむすびつく、
ことばも破片ばかりをひろいあつめる。
ぼくらの視野は
何ものもうつさぬ鏡
昆虫の死骸の散乱する平地に向う。

散乱する　イメジを収斂する
磁場を、〈場所〉を　求める
心の動きが精神というものか、
百人の難民のしるしづける視線
百人の星座。

《難民の目がこの世紀を支えている》

II

ことばは旗をもたない
ことばに　ぼくらが

123

われわれにとってのことば

I

頬のうえの　日の斑
ぼくらのしぐさは
まだ難民に似ている。
ぼくらには飢えた目が
渇いた口が依然としてよく似合う。

とおくの空で
兵器廠の幻がこわれる。
未来の都市の幻がこわれる。
反りかえったあぶり出しに
あらわれる姿。

死者に礼儀をはらうことに
ぼくらはまだ慣れない。
ぼくらには恐怖もわからない。
ことばがどれほどの空間を支えるか

久しい絶望、久しい虚構をみたすためには、そのためには、
一つの夜
一つの朝の、
さわやかな空気
青空の抜く手をみせぬ不意打ち、
ふきこぼれるガソリンのにおいのように鮮烈な
一つの出会いがあれば
じゅうぶんだ。

また笑いのうちに
ぼくを閉じこめ　ここからさき他所へはやるまいとし、
氷結しがちな心を溶かしてしまう。
ぼくらの出会うのはほとんど架空の市街、
しかも　このおそろしい
残酷さとやさしさを満載した街、
喧騒と静寂が隣りあう
底ぬけに明るく　また不幸な街。
"海賊"と"ギャング"どもに
虐殺されたブダペストとポートサイドの数万の声が、
そのままはねかえって
ぼくらを　たえず脅迫する街。
ビルに窓ガラス掃除人夫たちがゆっくりとのぼって行く
かわいた街だ。

一つのことは信じよう。
そのうえぼくは何を信じればいい？
くだかれたぼくらの心の

126

美しい唇　やさしい手　ぼくを
深い　おおきな湖に向きあわせる、
抱くことのできる　眼なのだから。
花々をおしひろげる球根のように
彼女の小さなのどは　今
ふるえていて、
そののどから　あふれ　はばたく
唾液は　光を紡いで
幾万羽もの　鳥になる。
今度はその鳥たちの　柔毛におおわれた
心臓が　めぐりめぐって
搏っている球根となる。

ふしぎにすべてが似かよってくる。
それはいい兆だ。
来ないとすれば　それは
呼ばないからだ。
彼女の湖は
ずっと遠くに夢みることあるをおしえ

その生命の色が
かがやくことによって似かよってくる。
生命の色は止どまることを欲しない。
それはまじわることによって完成する。
苦痛や悲しみの黒さえも　よろこびの
黄や赤や青の乱舞を支えるものとなる。
似かよってくる
それは一人の女に似かよってくる
一人の女が
すべてのものに似かよってくる。

その渦のなかに
しかめっ面した過去は
追跡者の証明書をなくしてしまう。
空虚な夜のひろがりが
否応なく明日の呼吸をさぐりはじめる。
世界は一人の女のうちに
もっともゆたかに発展し、
彼女はすでに

ふしぎにすべてが似かよってくる

ふしぎにすべてが似かよってくる。
それはいい徴だ。
雨に溶けあう森の色のように
隣りあわせに坐った　愛する二人が
難なくわかちあう
熱いそしてつめたい体温のように。
すべてが少しずつ　しだいに
交流しはじめる。
そんな時がやってくる。
それはそうねがうひとたちのところに
鳥を呼ぶ　木の枝ほどのたしかさで
やってくる。それらが
来ないとすれば　それはいつでも
呼ばないからだ。
似かよってくる。
それは火を点けられて

129

サン゠ポール・ド・ヴァンス

サン゠ポール・ド・ヴァンスの丘の上で
きみはいまひとりのご婦人と
ジャック・プレヴェールの話をする。
彼女はプレヴェールに
いい詩をつくってもらおうと
日本のすてきな紙をあげようとした
だがプレヴェールは　詩はトイレットペーパーに書きますと
彼女の申し出をことわった
いじわるでいけない人ね
でもすばらしいすてきな詩人
サン゠ポール・ド・ヴァンスに
プレヴェールはもう来ないらしい。

130

母と国と言語がある
母と国と言語から
切れていたと自分に言いきかせた半年間
わたしは傷つくことなく
現実のなかを歩いていた。
わたしには　詩を書く必要は
ほとんどなかった。

四月にパウル・ツェランが
セーヌ川に投身自殺をしたが、
ユダヤ人だったこの詩人のその行為が、
わたしにはわかる気がする。
詩とは悲しいものだ
詩とは国語を正すものだと言われるが
わたしにとってはそうではない
わたしは母国語で日々傷を負う
わたしは毎夜　もう一つの母国語へと
出発しなければならない
それがわたしに詩を書かせ　わたしをなおも存在させる。

母国語

外国に半年いたあいだ
詩を書きたいと
一度も思わなかった
わたしはわたしを忘れて
歩きまわっていた
なぜ詩を書かないのかとたずねられて
わたしはいつも答えることができなかった。

日本に帰って来ると
しばらくして
詩を書かずにいられなくなった
わたしには今
ようやく詩を書かずに歩けた
半年間のことがわかる。
わたしは母国語のなかに
また帰ってきたのだ。

母国語ということばのなかには

しゃがんでいたりする。

ついで彼女は
失くしてしまった空の方に
もっと澄んだのがあったとも云った。

切り抜かれた空

彼女は僕の見たことのない空を
蔵い込んでいる。
記憶の中の
幾枚かの切り抜かれた空。

時々階段を上って来て
大事そうに
一枚一枚を手渡してくれる。

空には一つの沼があって
そこには
いろいろなものが棲んでいると云う。

そこに一度きりしか通過したことのない
小さな木造の駅があって、
草履袋をもった
小学生が

おれたちには
わからない
それを思い描くことがたやすくは
できない
ただ手ずれた
大きなハンカチからとり出された
一本の匙が
無量のことばを告げ
とおく
あの年からきたと考えていた
おれたちをかぎりなく引戻す
一月の
日の光は
ただしずかにひろがり
木々はなおもざわめき　揺れやまない。

（一九六一年一月アウシュヴィッツの遺品をはじめて見て）

135

匙

焼け錆びた一本の匙が
日の光をいっそうまぶしいものとする
とても見ていられないほどのものにする
木々がざわめいている
この匙は
かつて一人の人間がそれで食物をたべたものである
かれがどんな顔をしていたかどんなことをしていたか
かれもおれたちも人間であるからには
おれたちは
それを
かんたんに類推することができる
かれが日の光を
まぶしがったり
木々のざわめきを愛しただろうことは
はっきりわかる
しかしかれをアウシュヴィッツで殺した者
がどんな人物だったか

136

いま　それ以上の　ことを
考えることができない
血のことを　考えるよりも
川のことを考える
ほうがよい

日本には　ついに
思想らしい思想は　生れないのか、
と悲しみながら

風の日の　しめ切った　あつい
電車に乗っている。
きみは悲劇的な
死者たちばかりを愛している。

137

きみは少しずつ　狂って行った。
人の顔が見られない。

12

日本中がテレビを囲んで　放心している。
テレビを見る練習をした一刻一刻
（きみがじいっとがまんして
生きては行けない
テレビをきらっていては

詩は　テレビに耐えて
必死になって　存在しようとしている。
（必死に　ということばは
好きではないが……）
夏の瘴気のなかに　じいっとしゃがんでいると、
そのことが　よく　わかる。

13

また　川を見に
行こう　と考える

138

軍服さえも　にせものだった
ぜったい本物の
鴎外のハイカラ
に　彼はひけ目を感じつづけたのである
彼は　にせものの軍服を着て
一切のテレビに反抗して
自滅した。
（自滅もできない男なんて　尊敬しても
好きには　なれない）。
彼は　正月の元旦のような気分が
一年中　ほしかったのだろう
あわれな男。

だが　いま文学などと言っている
どの連中よりも、
きみは三島のほうを　好きなのかもしれない。

三島の死のあと

別れぎわに
ピカソと肩を組んで
にこにこと笑っている
若い彼女の自慢の写真をくれた。
生きているときは
三島を　それほど好きではなかったのに、
いま　三島のことを
しきりに考える。
三島のいないいまになって。

彼はテレビに出て
まっ白な麻の服なんか着て
豪傑笑いなどしていたが、
ほんとはテレビもきらいだったにちがいない
テレビのあとの　こんなむなしさ
は耐えられなかった　にちがいない
その三島の気持は　よくわかる。
どんな立派な西洋館に住んでも
模造西洋に　すぎなかった

弟はいつも少し夢中になりすぎている。
木下サーカスには日中戦争のにおいがする。

11

テレビも夏も終って
考えることもなく、
三島由紀夫のことを考える。
高いベランダで　三島が死んだ日の夜
きみはニースから来た
ひとりの婦人と会っていた
その　いつも快活なおばあさんは
日本をよく知っている人である。
大森の　室内照明は完全なのに
何か暗い　ホテルの一室で
はじめて見る疲れた　暗い顔を
彼女はしていた
三島の死に方
と彼女は　くらいくらい顔をした。
ピカソの版画を見せてくれたが
ピカソもここでは暗かった

かかるジレンマの
絶えたることなし。

10

一九三九年夏
弟と木下サーカスを見に行った。
象……てんねんの、何とかというジンタ……
空中ブランコ、綱わたり
道化たち……天井の高くひろおい大テント
きみたちの国で　カテドラルの大天井に匹敵せんとするものは
あのテントだけである……
原っぱにサーカスのテントが張られると
行きも帰りも幸福だった
動物のにおい　　熱気　したたる汗
センベイ　キャラメル　コールコーヒー……
何よりもあの　象どもや　ライオンや　猿の
におい……しょうべんの太陽で煮つまった　におい……
（テレビのサーカスは
少しも　におわない）
きみは小学校の四年だった。

142

8

このころ　何をしたかは
一切　忘れたが、
歩いて二、三分の
川の明るさ、
だけは　はっきりとおぼえている。

9

気がかりが
ひとつあった

八月十日　陸軍航空士官学校から
八月二十日に入校せよ　との
電報がとどいていた。
もう行かなくてもいいにちがいないが、
行かないわけにもいかない
しかし行く必要はもうない
だが　行ってみたい気もしなくはない
戦後　最初のジレンマだった
それから三十年

143

S氏のことばのほうへと
いっさんに馳け出したのだ。

6

たしか八月十七日か八日
汽車に乗って
歩兵第十聯隊の兵営の門附近や
塀のまわりを歩いた
実にひっそりしている
ひっそりとして　人の気配はない
電信柱や　門のわきに貼られたビラに
《徹底抗戦！》という文字がある……。

7

駅はくさい
あの昭和二十年夏の　駅ほど
くさい場所を寡聞にして知らない
絶体絶命になると、
きれいな女もあのようにくさくなるのだ。

ラジオをとり囲んでいた。

みんな　黙りこくっていた
空だけが　上のほうにあった
まわりの人の顔が
見られなかった
泣くことも笑うこともない
とはあのことである。

突然　S医師が
銀行へ行って　金をおろして
来るようにと
奥さんに命じた
そのときのS氏のことばが
いつまでも
耳の底に
不快なものとして
残っていた
だが　いまは　そうばかりとも思わない
日本の戦後は

ような人に会わない
まして　大河をもっている
ような
人を見ずして久しい。

4

水をのむと
渇きは　癒える
しかし　それでも
癒やされない　渇きというものがある
その渇きだけは
確乎として　存在している
どこへでも
ついてくるのだ。

5

一九四五年夏
きみは　疎開先のN町の
S医院の　母屋の庭で　（母屋というものがあった）
S氏や　看護婦さんたちと

146

一つの車輌に
三人くらいしかいない
窓からの風に
この夏　ただ一度
の涼しさを　味わった
山あいの川が
見えはじめた
どこまでも　川はあった
自分のため　だけに　流れている
ほんものの　川だった

川は
この夏　見たもので
いちばん　立派な　存在だった。

　　　3

その川の　ことを
ときおり　思い出す
このごろ　川が
気になる
内部に　川をもっている

147

川と河

1

きみのみじめさは
内部に　大河をもっていない
ということに
尽きる。

言えることは
きみのみじめさは
内部に　大河をもっていない
ということだ。

2

この夏は一度だけ
川を見た
大泉から　池袋へ行かずに
西武秩父行きに乗った
まだ午前なので

曝らされているのは
一体何か
かすかな　しかししつこい不安が
帰る途じゅう　つづき
いまも　つづいている。

しつこい不安

きょう　マーケットの肉屋で
ミンチの器械を眺めていて
気持がわるくなった。
汗がじわりとにじみ
呼吸がくるしくなった。
すりつぶされているのは
われわれのなけなしの
空白な　内部ではないのか、
守るべき内部も
それほどあるわけではないが
それは　家のなかに
突然　汗まみれの
上半身裸の
電気工夫か　水道工事人が
入りこんできた
のに似ているようだ。

いったい何処へ飛んで行ってしまったのか。これからどうなるのだ。
アメリカよ　君が勝った日のおれたちの姿だ。

君たちの大統領が日米修好百年を記念して
日本へやってくる。羽田に下り立つかつての物体のために
おれたちも左手にスターズアンドストライプスを
右手に日の丸の小旗をもってうち振ろうか。
日本政府はかつてない歓迎の宴をはるだろうか。
日本人の多くは何となく　あくまでただ何となく
テレビにうつった第二次大戦の敵の勇将のすがたを
眺めるだろう。
おれたちも眺める。
ふきあげる埃りのなかでおれたちのすがたはかすむ。
行動することは
いつも誰かがやった。
いつも誰かがだ。
物干竿に何本ものおしめとナイロンがぶらさがり　きょうも
そのむこうにごったジュラルミン色の海が光っている。
物体の海だ。

151

気温も雨量も蝉の声も　はや
記憶からくっきりとぬけおちたが、
人々のひっそりと階段を上り下りするあしおと、
ひっそりとした話し声、
暗幕がとり外された
部屋のバアッとした明るさ、
月光色のヒマワリの林
は忘れられない。
父親はづだ袋を背負ってとおい鉱山の町から帰ってきた。
どすぐろく疲れた顔をして。
その表情もまわりの人とおなじだった。
父親はやがて困惑しはてたような笑いをもらした。
おれはそのとき何を考えていたのだろう。　航空適性検査の機械にはげしく振りまわ
され
平衡感覚をうしなって投げ出された自分の姿のことか、
白く埃りっぽい京都のほそい家並か低いひさしか
空倉庫のまえにバラバラッと立っていたヨモギ色の
朝鮮人の少年工のことだったか。
ぶっつりと切れたタコ糸のように終ってしまった戦争は

ポパイはやっぱりホーレン草を食べており、
物体がはき出したフィルムのなかで
アメリカはせっせと食べたり、歩いたり、恋愛したりしていた。

あれから十五年たちアメリカとおれたちとのあいだにも
さまざまの事件があった。今では
空を飛ぶ物体のなかにおれたちは人が乗っていることを
やすやすと想像できるようになった。
ちょっと見たところおれたちと少しもちがわない軍曹や曹長
しかしオキナワやパールハーバーやガダルカナルなど
いくつもの血だらけの地名がおれたちとアメリカとのあいだに
錆びついたピンでとめられていた。

アメ帝かえれ！　のビラも今は
きれいにホースの水で洗い流されふきとられた。
アメリカの水兵が何人か真冬の寒空にどぶんと投げこまれた、
数寄屋橋のどぶ川も埋められた。
だが　物体は今も空をキーンとよこぎり
テレビのブラウン管の影像を波形にし、
おれたちの神経をかきみだす。あの年の夏の

153

アメリカ交響楽

おれたちは勤労動員さきの
防空壕のなかにしゃがんで　はじめて
ジャズをきいた。安物のポータブルの口から
異国くさい旋律がガタガタときこえてきた。
そのうえをキーンと銀色に光った一点がB29で
空はどこまでも晴れていた。おれたちは
純粋に物体としてその一点を見あげていた。

物体は焼夷弾や機関銃弾を投下した。
あれがおれたちの戦さのおわりでおれたちは
ベークライトくさい麦飯ともおわかれだった。
物体は厚木に下りてそこからぞろぞろとGIたちがあらわれた。
物体がはき出したのは人間だった。
物体がはき出した人間のなかには陽気で善良な
ヤンキーがいた。
おれたちは『武器よさらば』をはじめて読んだ。
その響きのいいことばをおれたちもうれしげに口誦んだ。

他人の空

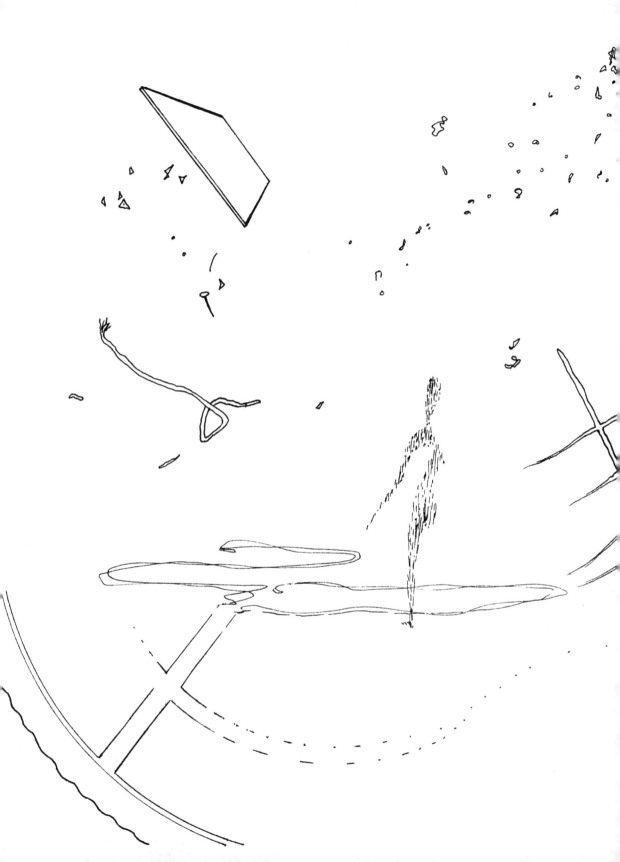

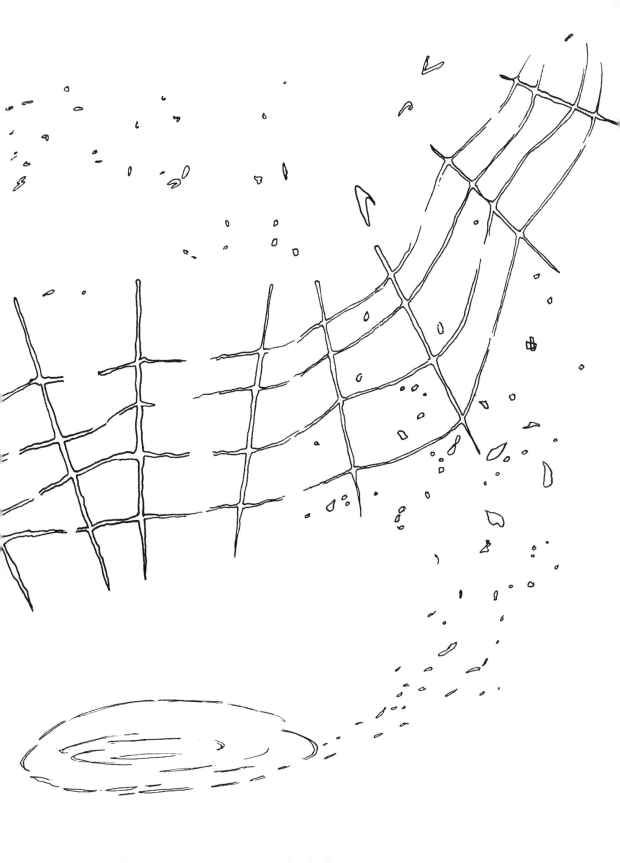

エロチックであり
礼儀正しい老人を眠らさぬ
ガーゼの月のなまめかしさで
老人は回想する
正確にいうならば創造するのだ
胃袋と膀胱のために
交代のない沙漠の夜を
はいえなや禿鷹の啼きごえを
星と沙の対等の市を
そして小舎の炎の中心に坐り
王者の心臓の器で
豪奢な血を沸騰させようとする
むなしく伏せられた
笊のごとき存在
みごとな裸の踊子も現われぬ
不安な毛の世界で
床屋の主人が剃刀をひらめかせ
老人の大頭を剃りあげる
石膏のつめたさ
美しい死者として
幼児とペリカンの守護神として
他人には邪魔にならぬ所へ移される

161

老人頌

さびしい裸の幼児とペリカンを
老人が連れている
病人の王者として死ぬ時のため
肉の徳性と心の孤立化を確認する
森の木の全体を鋸で挽き
川来るだけゆっくり
幽霊船を組立てる
それが寝巻の下から見えた
積込まれたのは欠けた歯ばかり
痔と肺患の故国より
老人は出てゆく
皮の下から続く深い波のうねりへ乗り
多毛の妻をうつぶせにする
黒い乳房の毒素で
人の心もさわがしくみだれ
くらげの体も蠢いている
老人は腹蔵なく笑う
ばんざい
ばんざい
一度は死も新しい経験だから
蝶番のはずれた境界を越える夜は
裂れぬ魚の腹はたえず発光し
たえず収縮し
そのうえ恐しく圧力を加えて

162

わが家の記念写真

おかあさんは腰巻きする人
首つりのタモの木にそってゆき
朝日はのぼる
島の墓原で
百羽のツグミを食う猛き人
それが義理あるおとうさんの暗き心
いやになるなあ
公園からとんでくる
ラグビーボールをスカートのなかへ
おねえさんは隠したままだ
なので寄宿の猫は
沼面を走る雨にぬれる
幽鬼のように
いもうとは善意の旅をしている
星ピカリする夜々を
みなさん揃いましたか
では記念写真をとりますよ
青空へむかって
にっこり笑って下さい
でもうまく映るだろうか
時すでにぼくは
地中海沿岸地方の奥地で
コルクの木とともに成長している

163

この氷い報復の難儀な旅の夜も明けよう
しきつめられた喪服の世界に
ピラミッドの頂点がわずかに見える
これほど集ってはじめて
全部の母親のさかまく髪のなかに
あたらしい空が起り
実数の星座が染められる

死児は見るだろう
未来の分娩図を
引き裂かれた血の闇の稲妻
その凄しい血の闇から
次々に白髪の死児が生まれ出る

Ⅷ

死児をだいて集る母親たち
或る廃都・或る半球から
おしきせの喪服のすそをひきずって
まれには償いの犬までつれ
定員になるまで沙漠へ入ってゆく
他のおしゃべりの母親たちは
沈黙を求められて村落から海面へ移動する
次から次へ黒い帯の宗教的なながれ
限りなくこの現世を司どるために
死児が生きかえらぬようにあやす
子守唄と悪夢のくりかえしで
骨肉でどうしてこの文明の腐敗の歌を合唱できよう
とどろく雷のように
豊かな腰をよじり
最後に半数のやもめの母親たちが氷河に並ぶ
必ず一人の死児をだいてる証拠に
めいめい死児の裸の臀を叩く
そのはげしさで哭いた時

死んだものは変換できないと
破船の家でどなりだす
死児は声が小さく主張できない
母親の目の届かぬ所に来て
氷ったまま横臥する
かたわらに
伝説の軌跡の海

Ⅶ

母親のねむった後
死児が床を這い廻る
果ては
春の嵐の海を埋めつくす
死者のうわむきの顔の上で立ち上り
次から次へと
跳ね歩く死児
凌辱された姉を求めて
ただ一人の姉でなく多くの姉の
波の魂に呼ばれて
陰気な蓮華をかざして行く
腿の柱をきよめに
混血の海へ
姉が孕み
姉が産む夥しい死児の夜の祝祭
輝く王道をきりひらき
古代の未開地で

166

大理石の死児
鉄線の黒い死児
金髪の森の死児あまたの砂の死児
そのとき
賢い母親は夏の蝉の樹木の地に
異なるエネルギーで
異なる泣き声で
同一の怒りの歴史をつくる

VI

死児の好きな遊び
むらがって
珊瑚の海へ網を入れる
大砲と共に沈んで行った男たちの重い睾丸をひびかせる
女たちの砂と闇を吸ってる肛門も色彩でかざる
死んだ者のためなら安心して仕事ができる
塩と金具の頬の枷をはずし
丈夫な膠でボデーをくるみあげ
枯木の陸地で二度目の奉公をかなえさせてやるんだ
ざくざく採れる金銀の鱗
さめの歯のかみあう恍惚の日々
水の夜伽は退屈だと静かな骨はつぶやく
死児にはそれが聴える
もう一度月から網を可能なかぎり拡げよう
死んだものならなんでも収穫
母親はいやな顔を見せて手伝わず

V

蠟びきの世界の首府を
母親は死児を背負って巡礼する

砕かれたもぐらの将軍
首のない馬の腸のとぐろまく夜の陣地
姦淫された少女のほそい股が見せる焼かれた屋根
朝の沼での兵士と死んだ魚の婚礼
巡艦は砲塔からくもの巣をかぶり
火夫の歯や爪が刻む海へ傾く

死児の悦ぶ風景だ
しかし母親の愛はすばやい
死児の手にする惨劇の玩具をとりあげる
死児には正しきしつけを
もしいやがるものは罰せよ
白昼の紳士淑女の食卓へ恥部を曝せ
夜戦のすきなあらゆる国の紋章を引裂いた髙みから
死児の髪を垂らし
或はつるつるの頭を露出する
辱しめよ
死んだ父・殺された同胞の肉体の辱しめと
魂の憂欝なばらを照らしめよ
死児が苦痛のあまり汚物をながすまで
箒の黄いろい死児

168

死児は世界中の死せる老人と同衾する
かぼちゃの花ざかり
去勢の噴水はきらめく
いまは緑の繻子の靴に踏まれる森の季候
できれば消滅の知識をまなぶ

Ⅳ

歴史家の墓地の菫で物語られる
死児は医者の記録にのこるのでなく
最後は霧の硝煙で消える
悪化の一途をたどり
食物と父の怯懦の関係で
死児の病気の経過は
夢を孕む内部へうずまく
死児の爪は外部へのびず
商人の老獪な算術が病気をつくる
秋の果物を河へ搬びすぎた
それ故この時世は呪術の岩の下をさまよう
硫黄の苦い結晶体
無理にのぞけば
不順な風土と暴力の下着にかくされて
母親の乳房はどこの地平にも見あたらぬ
蜜と海綿のみなもとを涸らす獣の跳梁
すべての医者は沈黙した
死児の発育と病気について

Ⅲ

死児は偶然見つける
世界中の寝台が
行儀よく老人を一人ずつ乗せて軋むのを
ゆるんだ数々の蛇口から
回虫が老人と死にみきりをつけ
はいだしてゆく方向に
野菜と肉の積まれた
働く胃袋が透視される
ときどき鉄砲の筒先が向けられて
悲鳴も聞えた
老人の浄福を祈り
ゆっくり山へ血を持ちはこび
頂から浴せる
因襲の恋人・夫婦たちの寝台に
ただ一つの理由で死児は哭く
セックスを所有しないので
回虫のごとく恥じる
いうなれば交情の暁
やわらかな絹の寝台
妻の畑の涼しい蔭の場所に住めぬ
死児は老いた母親の喪服のやみで
くりかえすひとりの乱行を
あらあらしい石の発芽を
禁制の増殖　断種の光栄

170

死児は棺の炎の中でなく
埋葬の泥の星の下でなく
生けるわれわれを見る側にいる

II

枯木ばかりの異国で
母親は死児のからだを洗う
中世の残忍な王の命令だ
全部の骨で王宮を組上げる
ほのおの使役の終り
母親の涙の肥てた土地を
馬のひずめにとじこめられて
死児のむれは去る
真狂は家来の悦ぶごうもんの時
一つの枯木に一人の母親を与える
枯木が殖えればその分だけ母親が木に吊られる
百万の枯木はよろめき百万の母を裂く
八月の空に子宮の懸崖
世界の母親のはげしい眼は見る
　　　　　山火事を
　　同時に聞く
　それを消しに来る大洪水を

171

死児

Ⅰ

大きなよだれかけの上に死児はいる
だれの敵でもなく
味方でもなく
死児は不老の家系をうけつぐ幽霊
もし人類が在ったとしたら人類ののろわれた記憶の荊冠
永遠の心と肉の悪臭
一度は母親の鏡と子宮に印された
美しい魂の汗の果物
だれにも奪われずに
父親と共に働き薬でつつまれる
地球の円の中の新しい歯
誠実な歪みのなかの堅固な臀
しかし今日から
死児は父親の義眼のものでなく
母親の愛撫の虎でなく
死児は幼児の兄弟でなく
ぶどう菌の寺院に
この凍る世紀が鐘で召集した
新しい人格
純粋な恐怖の貢物
裁く者・裁かれる者・見る者
みごとな同一性のフィルムが回転する

172

なめされた猿のトルソ
そよぐ死せる青い毛
ぬれた少年の肩が支えるものは
乳母の太股であるのか
猿のかくされた陰茎であるのか
大鏡のなかにそれはうつる
表意文字のように
夕焼は遠い円柱から染めてくる
消える波
褐色の巻貝の内部をめぐりめぐり
『歌』はうまれる
サフランの花の淡い紫
招く者があるとしたら
少年は岩棚をかけおりて
数ある仮死のなかから溺死の姿を藉りる
われわれは今しばらく　語らず
語るべからず
泳ぐ猿の迷信を——
天蓋を波が越える日までは

173

サフラン摘み

クレタの或る王宮の壁に
「サフラン摘み」と
呼ばれる華麗な壁画があるそうだ
そこでは　少年が四つんばいになって
サフランを摘んでいる
岩の間には碧い波がうずまき模様をくりかえす日々
だがわれわれにはうしろ姿しか見えない
少年の額に　もしも太陽が差したら
星形の塩が浮んでくる
割れた少年の尻が夕暮れの岬で
突き出山されるとき
われわれは　　一茎のサフランの花の香液のしたたりを認
める

波が来る　白い三角波
次に斬首された
美しい猿の首が飾られるであろう
目をとじた少年の闇深く入りこんだ
石英のような顔の上に
春の果実と魚で構成された
アルチンボルドの肖像画のように
腐敗してゆく　すべては
表面から
処女の肌もあらがいがたき夜の
エーゲ海の下の信仰と呪咀に

固い胸当のとりでを出る
生涯収穫がないので
世界より一段高い所で
首をつり共に唄う
されば
四人の骨は冬の木の太さのまま
縄のきれる時代まで死んでいる

気球の大きさのシーツ
死んだ一人がかついで干しにゆく
雨のなかの塔の上に

7
四人の僧侶
一人は寺院の由来と四人の来歴を誄く
一人は世界の花の女王達の生活を書く
一人は猿と斧と戦車の歴史を書く
一人は死んでいるので
他の者にかくれて
三人の記録をつぎつぎに焚く

8
四人の僧侶
一人は枯木の地に千人のかくし児を産んだ
一人は塩と月のない海に千人のかくし児を死なせた
一人は蛇とぶどうの絡まる秤の上で
死せる者千人の足生ける者千人の眼の衡量の等しいのに
慾く
一人は死んでいてなお病気
石塀の向うで咳をする

9
四人の僧侶

4

四人の僧侶
朝の苦行に出かける
一人は森へ鳥の姿でかりうどを迎えにゆく
一人は川へ魚の姿で女中の股をのぞきにゆく
一人は街から馬の姿で殺戮の器具を積んでくる
一人は死んでいるので鐘をうつ
四人一緒にかつて哄笑しない

5

四人の僧侶
畑で種子を播く
中の一人が誤って
子供の臀に蕪を供える
驚愕した陶器の顔の母親の口が
赭い泥の太陽を沈めた
非常に高いブランコに乗り
三人が合唱している
死んだ一人は
巣のからすの深い咽喉の中で声を出す

6

四人の僧侶
井戸のまわりにかがむ
洗濯物は山羊の陰嚢
洗いきれぬ月経帯
三人がかりでしぼりだす

四人がいっせいに立ちあがる
不具の四つのアンブレラ
美しい壁と天井張り
そこに穴があらわれ
雨がふりだす

3

四人の僧侶
夕べの食卓につく
手のながい一人がフォークを配る
いぼのある一人の手が酒を注ぐ
他の二人は手を見せず
今日の猫と
未来の女にさわりながら
同時に両方のボデーを具えた
毛深い像を二人の手が造り上げる
肉は骨を緊めるもの
肉は血に晒されるもの
二人は飽食のため肥り
二人は創造のためやせほそり

僧侶

1

四人の僧侶
庭園をそぞろ歩き
ときに黒い布を巻きあげる

榧の形
憎しみもなしに
若い女を叩く

こうもりが叫ぶまで
一人は食事をつくる
一人は罪人を探しにゆく
一人は自瀆
一人は女に殺される

2

四人の僧侶
めいめいの務めにはげむ
聖人形をおろし
磔に牝牛を掲げ
一人が一人の頭髪を剃り
死んだ一人が祈禱し
他の一人が棺をつくるとき
深夜の人里から,押しよせる分娩の洪水

179

暗が次元を替える　中心に自然の光の接触をくりかえす

二十世紀の庭に　ぼくは綜合体として健康な男の一人

になる　まず梨から食いはじめる　ここに新しい関係・

対話がはじまる

下痢

ぼくは下痢する　のぞむところでなく　拒む術もなく
歴史の変遷と個人の仕事の二重うつしの夜にまぎれて
ぼくは下痢する　紅いろの花と　薄明の空をそめる痰の
吐かれる地下室の水　それはぼくだけの現象だろうか
今日もそれをする昨日もしたんだ　考えれば昔の記憶の
なかの青い膚のとうがんの内房を覗きながら　下痢はぼ
くらの日常の習慣　洗いたての世界の便器が集められる
ぼくの下痢はぼくの精神を飲みくだし　他人の多くの
心へ伝達され　飢えの大衆の糧を腐らせてゆく　そのと
きから寝そべる老若男女のむれ　そのささやかな声　そ
のいじらしい手足の運動　それらの生きている証拠の排
泄の愛　誰もが流木の位置　ぼくはどこかもう少し高い
ところから　直接灰をかぶる　被虐的な食事をするため
馬や犬の経験もしないであろう　滑稽な形而上の下痢
をする　力なくむしろ生きることを認証する　痛みの導
くところ　帯の格闘の終りの空間に聳える塔をみる　ぼ
くの死すべき肉体の鳴りひびく殉教の血のながれがれの高ま
る時　ぼくは下痢する　耕される傾斜の土地に　汲まれ
る泉の絶えざる岩や石の下に　永久に心の内乱の契機の
腸を断つ　ぼくは忘れられる　ぼくは人と物を忘れる
仮設のなかにめぐりあった交友だから　寒冷な下痢する
近代の醜悪なかがまる催眠状態をぬけ　回復する驚異な

紡錘形 Ⅱ

わたしの生きている今　わたしは触っているのだ　それ
はずいぶん過去の年月の愛と羊水の水圧に抑えられたま
ま　小さな袋での一囲いの卵として　水平にねむり　立
った勢いでわたしは自分の足の爪を噛んだ　わたしの信
仰はそれから高まる　朝夕にくりかえされる食物の固形
の時　わたしはそのたび聴いた母性の甘い嘔吐を　もし
かしたら立ちあがれるかも知れない　ずいぶん狭い伽藍
だと思いながら　裸の姿で　いなむしろ裸以前のろうそ
くの形で　自分の投影を前後左右の壁に映しだす　これ
がこれが犬でないもの　鳥けものの羽を与えられぬもの
　呼称・父　呼称・母の夢みてる可憐な塑造の者　夜の
香料薬科のなかの血のアーチをくぐり出る　召命された
エキス　木造の首都で一市民のつづらのふたひらく四月
真綿をかぶり老婆が沐浴している

紡錘形 I

首のまがった母それはまだ女であり　見えない骨の走る
小さな父それは男であり　窓の外の地に死ねない人々が
めいめいの貧相な手で蠟をつみ　蠅をむらがらせ　哄笑
と泪声で　二人の男と女に寝床の時を与える　夜が鋭い
角をもつならば　他の人は畳の下へ沈む　火事は血を浴
び　母の子宮へ移りつつ燃える　父はもうつるつるの猿
として自己の枝へつりさがり叫ぶ　水を水を　母は鍋の
尻と箒で接がれた一つの化物に変り　襖の世界へ入って
ゆく　父は朝早くから桶のなかへ鍬形の手を涌し　労働
にたえる熱い鉄を打ちすえる　刻まれた錻の目が万の錐
の尖をとがらし　それらすべてが陰気な畳を突き刺す
それが生活であり　金銭であり　父はふいごの著しく長
い腹をよこたえる　母は障子の内側で孕みつつある

183

あまつさえ時間がくると滑る
それから先のぼくはまじめな森番だ
くさむらのひなを育てようと決意する
水べを渉る鷸のひなに変化した女の声を聴く
法律や煤煙のとどかぬ小屋で
卑俗なあらゆる食物から死守され
ぼくだけが攻めている美しい歯の城
その他の美しい武器をうばう
落日は輝くもの
おえつするもの
女の髪の上に滝が懸けられて凍る
ぼくは冷静に法典の黄金文体をよむ
さてぼくは女には大変つくした
罪深い女は去らせよう
ガス管工夫に肖た子をつれて桃の少女が結婚を迫るのを
ぼくは久しく待つんだ

熔接工はたちまちかにの形に歩き
総身の毛を輝かせ
充分な粘力と苦味のある泡を吹きこぼす
ところきらわずに
夫は岸べで焚火をたくばかり
破船と網の破れ目から
女が現われる
すなわち技師の妻が食物をはこんできて泳ぐ
熱い砂の床は人の心を複雑な巻貝に変化させ
同時に冷えた魚を跳ねまわす
その後での三人の食事は危険だ
皿やフォークが陰気にうごく
肉類や卵は食いつくされ
野菜類はつつましくのこる
海は死んだ男でふさがれる

6

ぼくは睡蓮の花を再びのぞく
転換が行われず
世界の女を巻く紐のすべてが解かれていない
蛙も挟まれる
花の深所から金髪が吹きだされるのを夢みる
ぼくは自分と不幸な女を救済すべく
女の腿へ手をのべる
喪服は夜に紛れやすい形と色を持つ

じゃがいもの麻袋をかるがると担ぐ情夫
人でなければ別のもの
頭の大きなさんしょううおを刺してきたのだ

4

永年の経験からぼくは被告を裏切る
被告はつねに救えぬ性格をもつから
彼らはすべて罰せられるにふさわしい陳述をする
例えばぼくが家具化した法廷につれこまれ
被告として黒服の者たちにとりまかれる
〈わたしの妻は蟻の世界へ亮渡される
溶けるもの　かがやく裸形の砂糖の袋〉と口走る
人々の心証を害し
それでぼくも犯罪人の両肩を見せ下獄する
ぼくの弁護人は妻子と両親のため家へ急ぐ
尻の袋にぎっしり穀粒をつめ脂がのった鶏の首をさげて
雨の中へ入る
不運な者は針金で養われ暗い所にいる

5

女の夫は老練な海港技師
熔接工を連れて毎日海へ行く
長い年月を海の下ではたらくので
真昼の光線に当るとき

186

悪い季候のはじまり
薄い皮の下で少女は変化している
花の植物の冠から
えびの姿態の不透明な袋に黒い汁を移しはじめる
ぼくの鼻毛の茂みを雨でぬれた鳥がとおりぬけるのはそ
んなとき
棚のあらゆる口の細い罎
液体を溜める闇のなかで
痙走感におののきだす
ぼくの寛容な肉情の下に在る
ぼくはいかなる変化
いかなる交換を待っているのか

3

ぼくの眠りの裁面がめのうのように滑らかになる
そこに居合せたただ一人の女
喪服にいつわられた美しい肢体の女が昨日からいる
今は組みあげられた脚線として
ぼくの寛容な肉情の下に在る
朝から使役された上半身
殊に肩の裏の可憐なそばかすの星璽
恐しくぼくの頭を捉える
或る瞬間は照らす
察するところ女は人を殺してきたらしい
もし病弱な夫でなければ

感傷

1

鎧戸をおろす
ぼくには常人の習慣がない
精神まで鉄の板が囲いにくる
街を通るガス管工夫が偶然みて記憶する
箱のなかに匿れた一人の男
便器にまたがるぼくをあざわらう
桃をたべる少女はうしろむき
帽子をまぶかくかぶるガス管工夫の槌の一撃を憎む
少女の桃を水道で洗わせず
狭い蜜のみなもとを涸していったから
幼い袋の時代
大人の女の汗の夏を知らぬ
少女もいつかは駆けこむだろう
ぼくの箱の家
正面の法律事務所の畸型の入口の柱を抱くだろう
それまで休業だ
屋根から寝台まで縞馬を走らせ
ペンキを塗り廻る
すでに伽藍の暗さ

2

金魚鉢の水の上で睡蓮が咲く

188

馬・春の絵

わたしはそのとき競馬場の芝生にねて　円柱球の馬を見
ている　一二回跳ねるのを見た！　もしかりにわたしの
家の戸棚のなかに　馬が死んでいると確認したら　どれ
ほどわたしを悦ばせることか　わたしは早速そのスポン
ジ化した馬の臀を両手で抑える　それは夜まで続く　不
惑の人生をかえりみて　少数者の自由を守ろうと思う
戸棚からころがりだす酒盛と血まみれのハンドル　終り
に孔のたくさんある鉄の筒の胴廻りを計る　水に打たれ
て仲縮度を加える馬の首　それはわたしにとっては過ぎ
た戦いの心の忠部だ　それが女の首と太さが同等だった
時のわたしのおどろき　リンゴのように半分囓られた星
の下で　隣人みんなの哀れみを受ける　裂かれたカンパ
スよりもっと永遠でない闇から　愛撫する馬の腹へ　わ
たしは口をつけて囁く　《人間の幸福は各個人の生得の
もの》　女は蹄鉄の下からスカートをつける　ピンクと
グレーのゆるやかなカーブの藪の道へ帰って行く　わた
しはだれにも聞けないのだ　女は死んだ馬なのか　雨の
なかでいまでも跳ねる　かつてわたしが光で見た円柱球
の馬なのか　朝がきたらしいああいちじるしいナツメの
実　わたしは歯刷子で歯をみがき　それを取りおとすだ
ろう　世界はいつも余分なものをつくり　わたしに余分
な仕事を与える

伝説

椅子の上から　跳びおりてゆく　猫の毛のなかの跣足
刹那のことだが　大写しになり　花の深いひだに　吸い
こまれた　誰でもが初めてのことだと驚く　木製の四つ
の脚　床をしばらく跛行し　部屋の隅で急に停止し　椅
子は伝説化された　事件を知らぬ男　かぶった毛布から
現われ　椅子にこしかける　流通する熱と臭気をぬきな
がら　肛門につながる管をけんめいにたぐり出す　抑え
きれぬゴムの状態で　かさばりはじめ　部屋中を占めて
のたうちまわる　ものの鼓動　快楽の伸縮　夜のため
その男は久しい前から　猫と顔をならべ　管にかこまれ
たまま　暗くなってゆき　息をころしてゆき　消える間
際で　火事だと叫んだ

190

チャリーの道具はどれも小さく
だれもが持っている日常性から
非日常性へオクタアブが替る
魔物芸術
チャリーの反商業主義の勝利だろうか？
サース・キャニオンの他の人の物干場から
とおく見える慰めの夜の火柱
チャリーは逃げることを拒否する
むしろ訪れる
むしろ静止
岩のセミの出来のわるい眼
見ることを禁じよ
生きる悦びの黒い枝々
牛乳しぼりの女と鳥がゆっくりと行なう
美しい死方
煙たなびく彼方の花嫁衣装
チャリーは頭の中の火
もえる襞　自己の火を消している
《外出のときは　雨具をおわすれなく》
《外出のときは　雨具をおわすれなく》
やさしい男チャリー・コルデン
亀甲のなかへの精射

191

カマスに喰われるイワシの毒性のない肉質

肥っていることが罪なら

チャリーの体重は零

頭は燃えるアメリカネズミの尾

火縄の円

ぐるぐる廻っているんだ

それは電気よりも精神的なもの

チャリーの呪う心は皮をはがれたウサギのように

他の人の厚塗りの人類愛からはみだして

けいれんする絵画

公衆を冷笑する

患部でなく全体的患部

他の人の観察できない

蜜蠟の赤

チャリーの逃げる劇

ひとつの鉄の柱から他の柱へ

アメリカの高層気流から

シナのさかれたフカの水墨の海へ

逃げるチャリーが見えるか？

他の人の心はマッチが擦られるほど熱くない

しかし今日この午後でも

やさしい放火魔チャリー・コルデンの

よだれは熱くしたたる

あらゆる現実の森林は火を産むさびしいしとねだ

タバコ・フィルター・セルロイドの函

やさしい放火魔

夏ははげ頭なんか刈りたくないと
チャリーはいつも思う
まして少女のうぶ毛の口のまわりを
剃りたくないと考える
ミルクのみ人形の腹のように
いやらしい雨期をおもわせるんだ
理髪師チャリーは毎日
冷蔵庫の白い肌をふいていたいと思う
それはすきな消防車の鏡のように
爆発しそうな内臓をしている
猫へやる魚が死んでならび
コカ・コーラのビンはガチガチ鳴る
チャリーの求めてる冷たい水と
凍った不定形な涙
かつて少年だった記憶もなく
彼の記録は森林放火十四回
三十二才のチャリーは悲鳴をあげ
血のうえに母と妹をカモメのように
飛ばせている
それから停電のなかの滑車の下降
永劫に新しい戦争写真
艶のはえていることが大人なら
チャリーは酢の中の大人

193

単純

警戒もされずにその男は死んだ　尾骶骨のいちじるしく
突起した男に　妻は憎しみしかもたず　眼のかわりに舌が
つめたくかがやくので　乳房のゆたかな女である妻には
たえられぬ　食事するとき以外は　うごきが非常にかん
まんだ　むしろないといえる　ことに就寝するとき　植
物の花をつけぬ部分を感じさせ　地に伏してゆく陰惨な形態をとる
とにひっぱられて
しかし死んだ妻にはそれはどうでもよい　ただ毎日たえ
ず波うつ手で　壁の向うに飼っている犬に餌を与える
その偽証が心から妻を死なせないのだ　じぶんの美質を
うけつぐ猫が屋根で雪をかぶり　生きていることがはが
ゆい　もしじぶんの蛇腹が暗の裡から充分のび　男の歩
きまわる部屋へ突き戻せたら　勝目はある　石膏の胎児
を孕めるから　犬は男の身のまわりのせわをやき　困ら
せたり笑わせる　それからさきの甘美な操作はできぬ
男は生きるためには　死んだ妻の猫を鷹ばかりふる屋根
から呼び戻して　芸を仕込まねばならぬと考える　世俗
的な事柄でなく　美しい女に仕立てあげ　最初の夜は寝
台であたためて　溺死者の好む月をのぼらす　裸の女の
姿勢と葉の下に息づく桃の半熟の羞恥を　えとくさせる
べく大声をだした　夏がきた稲妻の紐をたらして　男は
人間である証拠のゆえに死ぬのか　頭は犬の血をさわが
せ　下半身は猫の毛に被われたまま　汗の強国から　肌
寒い一寒村へと葬られた

喜劇

台所の隅で　背中を裂かれた卵が泛び上る　長い夜の岸
に近く　眠っていた一人の男が立ちあがった　肩に一四
の帽子をかぶった猫をのせて　男は死んでゆく妻のため
に穴をほる　食物と金をつんだ手押車が反対に出てゆく
その道筋をふさぐ寝台の脚と什器類　男が突きながら
なでるため猫の咽喉から葡萄状にねずみの姿は溶け
正面の月を消す　遠くから向きをかえる森の樹　やがて
雪をかぶり　小さな部屋へ男と斜視の眼の猫を呼び戻す
だが歩くことはない　元から煖炉の前で男はグラスに
酒を注ぎ　猫は屋根裏を走っていたのだから　寒がりの
男は脱毛する猫をねらう　完全な裸の猫のまぶしさに男
は眼をふせる　その夜の窓をのぞく鳥はどれも　死んだ
妻の髪のかたちをするので射ち落す　男はおもむろに猫
の四肢を解く　その波の手の没するのは黄色を増したバ
ターの壺　危険な培養に魅了され　医者の指をつけ男は
汗をながす　思わず猫はグラスを砕く　その時たしかに
男は救われたのだろう　噴霧器のなかの指はアミーバの
昂進を止め　人間の手に退化したのだから　そのうえ破
片の間から輝く血をながした　重い物を支えたくなった
のだろう　男はあたりを見まわし　鋲や固い家具にとり
まかれていたのに驚く　それからは傷つかぬ部分　足や
顔や性器を急に大切に取扱う　丈夫な皮の袋から　男は
二度と現われぬ

195

水は起伏してながれる　透明な世界では悦びもなく射
精は終る　すぐそばにタコのメスのみひらかれた眼があ
る　それには汎神論的な悪意が感じられる　受胎せるタ
コのメスは海の底の石の巣へゆっくり帰って行く　二十
万粒の透明な卵を生むために　それから絶食状態のまま
ブドウの房のようにたれさがった袋の卵群へ　必死に
泡を吹きつづける　それは呼吸に必要な酸素を送るため
だ　ゆらぐ海草のかげで　タコの母親はただ一度の排卵
で腐る肉質へと替る

＊

ひとりの女が悪い想像からうまれるように
塩と水からタコは出現したのだ
漆黒の抽象絵画
砂は砂によって埋まり
貝は内部で生きる
それは過去のことかも知れない
夏の沖から泳ぐ女がくる

タコ

*

火をへだてて呼びかける
やさしいタコの母親は藻をまさぐり
サンゴの棚にたれさがって
下を向く
フジツボの信仰深い孔へ
青びかりした累卵を送りこまんとする
そのそばに船長の屍体が
官能的に横たわっているときは
八点鐘を打つ
それからはじめて
タコの母親はとりみだした恋人のように
動く岩を抱く

*

タコの生殖はとても呪われたフォームを見せる　それは
濡れて裂かれた傘のような肉の散乱にちかい　タコのオ
スの七つの足は水を抱きこむ　そして残されたごく先細
りの一つの足がくだの器官の役目をする　ちょっと見る
と靴の紐のようにみすぼらしく　タコのメスの小さな
孔を探し求めて入りこむ　これが交接といえるだろうか

てあせる　もろい下の躰の管をすすむ血の粗い無責任な
軍隊を見すごす　そこでぼくは街を出る　風がぼくを氷
る人・滑る物に替える　だからぼくはつねに笑わず　さ
ようならもしない

固形

ぼくの偏見は多くの人をこまらす　ときに植物の茎とい
う茎へ剃刀を当てる　切口から展開される　悲劇的なば
ら色の育たぬ家族を見つける　水ものまず　光も咥える
ことのできぬ　薄い膜の男女　かすかな交接のひびき
花粉は壁や寝具を汚す　さわると固いざらざらの粒に近
い　それゆえ子供は玩具の車の世界を走らぬ　遊び場は
母の子宮　日蔭のへちまの棚の下　そこで滑る　ぼくは
すたすた田園を出る　ぼくの信条は　物は固形ですわり
よくあらねばならぬと考える　立てかけられた筏へ同時
に迫るぼくと一匹のとんぼの複眼　ぼくは余す所なく
ランニング姿の全身を写し　段違いの虹や山嶽の氷の錐
を背負う　あらゆるやわらかい蛙がきらいだ　固い羽
固い雨なら両手で愛撫する　試みに一つの壜を蹴る　人
が信ぜられぬほど　ぼくは恍惚として街に入る　攻撃さ
れた寺院の外側の石塀を叩く　これこそ上等の遊戯だ
病院へゆく若い妊婦のあとをつける　だんだん坂をのぼ
り石の縞目が中心へ向き　細い線を描いてゆき　がまん
できないすべすべの頂点で　白い腹を見せる　医者の笑
う時だ　鐘が乱打される火事の夕刻　鉗子やうごく鋏が
皮膚をのばし　袋の中身の頭をむかえにゆく　ぬるい種
子のたんぽぽの周囲は　痛みをつけてむしられる　脂肪
が清潔なランニングをふきつける　ぼくは頂の固形をみ

静物

夜の器の硬い面の内で
あざやかさを増してくる
秋のくだもの
りんごや梨やぶどうの類
それぞれは
かさなったままの姿勢で
眠りへ
ひとつの諧調へ
大いなる音楽へと沿うてゆく
めいめいの最も深いところへ至り
核はおもむろによこたわる
そのまわりを
めぐる豊かな腐爛の時間
いま死者の歯のまえで
石のように発しない
それらのくだものの類は
いよいよ重みを加える
深い器のなかで
この夜の仮象の裡で
ときに
大きくかたむく

闇の祝祭

闇の祝祭

吉岡実

化人の空

飯島耕一

Celebration In Darkness

Strangers' Sky

The Poems in Japanese

DATE DUE